THE COFFEE SHOP

"La Bottega del Caffé"

BIOGRAPHY

ROBERT CORNTHWAITE was born in St. Helens, Oregon, went through grammar and high school in Portland, and completed his formal education at the University of Southern California. By that time a war had intervened and the U.S. and Royal Air Forces had escorted him around the Mediterranean for three fascinating years.

After the war he went back into radio. Films followed in 1950. That year he appeared in six features, including a lead in Howard Hawks' *The Thing*. Nineteen-fifty was also the year he became a Blackfoot Indian. He was adopted into the tribe by Chief Joe Iron Pipe, dressed in feathers and speaking Sioux, all for the greater glory of RKO. More than sixty feature films have ensued, hundreds of play productions and even more episodes of television, perhaps most memorably as the demented mayor on *Picket Fences* who died nude on a rocking horse.

Mr. Cornthwaite's translations of Pirandello have played at the Arena Stage, Washington, D.C.; Oregon Shakespeare Festival, Ashland and Portland; Seattle Repertory; East West Players, Los Angeles; San José; Niagara-on-the-Lake; and several other regional theaters around the U.S. and Canada as well as the Roundabout in New York.

THE COFFEE SHOP
by Carlo Goldoni

translated by Robert Cornthwaite

Great Translations for Actors

SK
A Smith and Kraus Book

A Smith and Kraus Book
Published by Smith and Kraus, Inc.

Copyright © 1995 by Smith and Kraus, Inc.
All rights reserved

Manufactured in the United States of America

Cover and Text Design by Julia Hill

First Edition: August 1995
10 9 8 7 6 5 4 3 2 1

Library of Congress Cataloguing-in-Publication Data

Goldoni, Carlo, 1707-1793.
    [Bottega del caffè. English]
    The Coffee Shop
          p. cm. -- (Great translations for actors series)
    ISBN 1-57527-004-7
    I. Cornthwaite, Robert, 1917- . II. Title. III. Series.
    PQ4695.E5B6   1995
    852'.6--dc20   95-32904
                            CIP

Contents

Foreword

More than two centuries after his death, Carlo Goldoni (1707-1793) is alive and well. Just ask students of literature and people of the theater.

In Goldoni's lifetime the disputes about him were bitter. His critics scolded him for

> "having entered too freely into the sanctuary of refined amorous intrigue and unveiled its mysteries to the profane eyes of the common herd" (Albergati Capacelli, quoted by Guido Davico Bonino on page vii of Volume I, *Carlo Goldoni: Commedie,* Garzanti, 1987)

or having gone

> "fishing among servants and shopkeepers and shady characters for a model for the man of honor."
> (Baretti, ibid.)

His supporters, turning this view upside down, saw in the acuteness of Goldoni's realism a healthy dose of moral rigor. According to Pietro Verri,

> "in the comedies of Signor Goldoni the essence is a foundation of real virtue, humanity, benevolence, love of duty." (Ibid.)

Critics also disagreed about the form his writing took. According to Carlo Gozzi, a rival playwright, Goldoni should be listed

> "in the catalogue of the clumsiest, lowest, and most incorrect writers of our idiom" (ibid.)

while Gozzi's brother Gasparo praises Goldoni's style as

> "cultivated and free of vulgar expressions and idioms."
> (Ibid.)

You pays your money and you takes your pick.

* * *

Of one thing there is no doubt: Goldoni was a late bloomer. It might be more accurate to say that he bloomed and wilted, and bloomed and wilted yet again and again. At fourteen he ran away with a boatload of actors, but his father put him back in school. He studied law, which he disliked; nevertheless, when he grew up and married he frequently had to rely upon legal practice to feed himself and his family. Even in his playwriting he found he had to fall back on the old commedia dell'arte maskcharacters, long in decline, if he wanted to market his plays.

It was not until he was past forty that he was able to come into his own. In 1749 the *capocomico* or actor-manager Girolamo (sometimes spelled Gerolamo) Medebach of the Teatro Sant 'Angelo in Venice offered him a four-year contract that obligated Goldoni to write eight comedies and two melodramas for each theatrical season, beginning that autumn. It was a heavy and arduous schedule but it offered relative economic ease and it was steady. As a permanent resident in Venice for at least the next four years, Goldoni would no longer be starting and stopping and starting and stopping all over the map of northern Italy.

* * *

What was it like at this period in Venice, the great *Repubblica Serenissima*? First of all it is well to bear in mind that the word *repubblica* has a double meaning in Italian: 1. republic or commonwealth, and 2. confusion, disorder, mess, anarchy. (See the *Cambridge-Signorelli Dizionario*.) Guido Davico Bonino says in his historical-critical profile of Goldoni (op. cit. page xxxi):

> "The Venetian middle class of the 1750's lives in prosperity, yes...content with its immediate well-being, a

little mad in its obsession with the domestic proprieties, distracted or indifferent toward any obligations to society as a whole."

Meanwhile the great expansion of Venetian commerce, which in glittering years of past glory saw ships of the *Serenissima* push as far as the West Indies, had gradually dwindled.

"Reduced to a 'local' circuit (which includes at the most the Adriatic and the Mediterranean) the shipping traffic is atrophying. But it is above all the lack of boldness in projecting a different future for themselves (taking advantage of the decades of contact with the modern cultures of Europe) that precludes the merchant class from finding new markets and outlets (for example, such as the modernization of agriculture might make possible by rescuing farms from the oppressive control of aristocratic landowners through adequate financing)." (Ibid.)

It is this provincialism, this limited horizon, that forms the background of *The Coffee Shop*. Later this same provincialism, which thinks itself broad-minded because it imports Parisian fashions, will be brought to the fore in the *Villeggiatura* trilogy.

* * *

In Venice Goldoni began the long task of reforming Italian comedy. Central to his reform was the creation of characters in the fullness of actual life, warts and all, in a historical and social context clearly defined, closer to the common people than to the upper classes. It wasn't that he hated commedia dell'arte. He actually liked its perfected mechanics, its meshing theatrical gears, its possibilities for quick changes. But he was tired of the exasperating monotony of the "types," each frozen in a mask incapable of the constant flow of fleeting expression characteristic of real human beings and equally incapable of suggesting even faintly a believable individual belonging to a particular social class in a certain place at a certain time.

His goal was to bring the real world into the theater. Instead of the mask-characters of commedia dell'arte—the miser, the braggart warrior, the pedant, the clowns, the young lovers, all of them stock figures almost unchanged since the days of the Greeks and Romans—Goldoni wanted to bring real people of his own day into his plays. He wanted to individualize the personality of his characters, stripping away the conventional masks and placing these highly differentiated individuals in a real setting, both physical and spiritual.

Eventually he succeeded, but it was not a continuous ascent. On the contrary, his climb was interrupted by clusters of mediocre plays and lapses in taste, followed by resurgences of dazzling success.

The fact that many of the people in his plays were not rich or aristocratic personages but servants and fishermen and their womenfolk elicited scalding criticism. On the other hand, the innovation also brought Goldoni popularity at the box office. A broader audience was coming to the theater.

At the end of the first season, which had seen some difficult moments—skin-of-our-teeth successes like *L'avvocato veneziano* (*The Venetian Lawyer*), and outright failures like *L'erede fortunata* (*The Lucky Heiress*)— Goldoni had his leading lady Teodora Raffi, Medebach's wife, announce to their public that during the next season (1750-1751) her favorite author would honor them all with a good sixteen brand new comedies. Count 'em, sixteen.

It was a promotional ploy, and premeditated. By sweetening the pot with eight more plays than the contract called for, the theater stood a good chance of attracting a new public—and placating a *capocomico* and other actors always ready to desert at the first sign of a dwindling audience, a lowered box-office take, and the possibility of no pay after the last curtain.

Goldoni delivered on his promise. There were sixteen new comedies the next season, not all of them good. Four, however, were excellent. And one of these was *The Coffee Shop*.

* * *

Conceived at Venice, written at Mantua in April 1750, this comedy was performed for the the first time in the latter city on 2 May of the same year by the Medebach company

"to the most fortunate reception." (Ibid.)

In Milan it was a great success and later, between autumn and the carnival, at the Teatro Sant'Angelo in Venice it had twelve successive performances—a hit in those days.

In 1736 Goldoni had roughed in an early draft of *The Coffee Shop* in an intermezzo called *La bottega da caffè*, set to music perhaps by Vivaldi. The later comedy (*La bottega del caffè*) which he wrote in 1750 and staged first in Mantua, contained—among others—five characters speaking the Venetian dialect. For the first publication of this comedy in a collection of his plays (Paperini, volume I, 1753) Goldoni turned the dialect into the *lingua pura* or Tuscan, the official Italian language of today. He also did away with the traditional commedia masks. Brighella was renamed Ridolfo, and Arlecchino became Trappola.

Revived several times in the course of the nineteenth century, often under the title of *The Slanderer* (or *Backbiter*, or *Scandalmonger*) *at the Coffee Shop*, it has often been staged with notable success in recent times. In April 1924 it was played at the Teatro Alfieri of Florence by the company of Giuseppe Zago; in July 1934 it was performed at Venice in the courtyard of the Teatro San Luca by the company of the *Biennale* celebration with Raffaele Viviani under the direction of Gino Rocca; in April 1951 Memo Benassi revived it, with Alessandro Brissoni directing, at the Festival of the Teatro di Bologna; and five years later Benassi played it again with the Repertory Theater of Trieste under the direction of Cesare Vico Ludovici.

* * *

In his introduction to *The Coffee Shop*, Goldoni says to the reader (*L'autore a chi legge*):

> "When I first composed this comedy I did it with
> Brighella and Arlecchino included in the cast and had, truth
> to tell, the happiest reception from all sides. That success
> notwithstanding, in giving it over for publication, I believed I
> could better serve the Public by making it more universal,
> changing into the Tuscan speech not only the lines of the two
> Characters mentioned but also three others who spoke in the
> Venetian dialect.

"In Florence there appeared a comedy that was similar to this one of mine in title and in plot, the reason being that both were copied from my play. A friend with talent and wit and enterprise had put his memory to work but, having seen my play performed in Milan only once or twice, he had of necessity to insert many things of his own invention and mingle them in as best he could. I looked upon it as a joke of the kind one friend plays on another, and I have praised its cleverness; nevertheless, I neither wish to claim the good things in it that are not mine, nor do I wish that anything I disapprove of should pass for my own.

"For these reasons I have wished to inform the Public of this fact so that in comparing my play, which I now commit to print, with that of the aforementioned friend the truth may appear, and each one profit from his portion of the praise and be content with his portion of the blame.

"This Comedy has characters so universal that in every place it has been presented these characters were believed to be copied from local and easily recognizable originals. The Slanderer in particular has his prototype everywhere; and at times, though innocent, I have had to suffer the accusation of having maliciously copied him from an original they all recognized. No, absolutely; I am not capable of doing a thing like that.

"My characters are human, they are lifelike, and possibly true; but I draw them from the universal crowd of mankind, and chance will have it that some individual among them may recognize himself. When this happens, it is not my fault if the wretched character I drew resembles that particular wicked individual; no, it's the fault of the wicked individual that from the character I depict he finds himself by his own misadventure tarred with the same brush."

* * *

Quotations throughout this foreword have been rendered into English by the translator.

—*Robert Cornthwaite*

Characters

IN THE ORDER OF SPEAKING:

Ridolfo, owner of the coffee shop
Trappola, a waiter in the coffee shop
Giovanni, another waiter
Pandolfo, owner of the gambling parlor
Don Marzio, a Neapolitan
Eugenio, a cloth merchant
The barber's apprentice
Lisaura, a dancer
Flaminio, calling himself Count Leandro
Placida, wife of Flaminio, dressed as a pilgrim
Vittoria, wife of Eugenio
A waiter at the inn
Chief Constable

NON-SPEAKING:

Other constables
Other waiters

* * *

Time: Carnival season, 1750

Place: Venice

The Coffee Shop

ACT I

Scene: A piazzetta or rather a wide street with three shops—in the middle a coffee shop, to the right a wig and barber shop, to the left a gambling parlor. Above them are rooms with windows opening on the street. To the side of the barber shop is the home of Lisaura the dancer, and to the side of the gambling parlor we see the door and windows of the inn.

At rise: Ridolfo, Trappola, and Giovanni in front of the coffee shop.

RIDOLFO: Look lively, boys. Remember—snappy service with a smile.

TRAPPOLA: This getting up early is getting me down. And no customers yet. We could have slept another hour.

RIDOLFO: Any minute they'll come pouring in. It's not so early. The barber's open—see, he's dressing wigs—even the gambling house is already open.

TRAPPOLA: Oh, that joint—it's been open all night.

RIDOLFO: Pandolfo must make a killing.

TRAPPOLA: That dog always gets the meatiest bone. He marks the cards; he cheats the customers... Money goes in his door and never comes out.

RIDOLFO: Don't envy him; his chickens will come home to roost. Go roast some coffee and make a fresh pot.

TRAPPOLA: Do I put in the grounds from last night?

RIDOLFO: No! Make it properly!

TRAPPOLA: Boss, when was it you opened this shop?

RIDOLFO: You know—eight months ago.

TRAPPOLA: It's time for a change.

RIDOLFO: What do you mean?

TRAPPOLA: When a new shop opens—great coffee. After six months at the most—hot water and dregs. *(He leaves.)*

RIDOLFO: He's a joker. He'll keep the customers laughing and coming back for more.

(Pandolfo comes out of his gambling parlor, rubbing his eyes sleepily.)

Pandolfo—some coffee?

PANDOLFO: Please.

RIDOLFO: Giovanni, bring some coffee for Messer Pandolfo. *(to Pandolfo)* Sit down and make yourself comfortable.

PANDOLFO: No, no, I'm in a hurry. I have to get back to business.

Act 1

(Giovanni brings Pandolfo his coffee.)

RIDOLFO: Are they still gambling at your place?

PANDOLFO: Harder than ever. This game's been going on since yesterday.

RIDOLFO: Who's winning?

PANDOLFO: Me for one.

RIDOLFO: Have you been gambling with them?

PANDOLFO: I played a few hands.

RIDOLFO: My friend, the owner should stay out of the game. If he loses, the customers laugh at him; and if he wins, they're suspicious.

PANDOLFO: I don't care. It's not my fault I'm lucky!

RIDOLFO: Was Signor Eugenio gambling last night?

PANDOLFO: He's still at it. He hasn't eaten, he hasn't slept, and he's out of money.

RIDOLFO: Poor fellow! How much has he lost?

PANDOLFO: A hundred in cash, and now he's in the hole.

RIDOLFO: Who's winning?

PANDOLFO: The Count.

RIDOLFO: The Count? That cardsharp? Who else is playing?

PANDOLFO: It's down to the two of them.

RIDOLFO: Poor Signor Eugenio! He'll be ruined.

PANDOLFO: Who cares as long as the house gets its cut?

RIDOLFO: I wouldn't run a gambling house for all the money in the world…and watch people ruin themselves.

PANDOLFO: Friend, if you're that thin-skinned you'll never get rich.

RIDOLFO: That's all right. An honest living is enough for me.

(From inside the gambling parlor come calls for "Cards, more cards!" Pandolfo calls back to them:)

PANDOLFO: Be right with you!

RIDOLFO: Try to get poor Signor Eugenio away from that gambling table.

PANDOLFO: He can lose his shirt for all I care. *(He walks toward his shop.)*

RIDOLFO: *(calling)* Shall I put your coffee on the tab?

PANDOLFO: I'll match you for it.

RIDOLFO: I'm not a sucker, friend.

PANDOLFO: Don't be a cheapskate. My clients bring a lot of business to your shop, and you're worrying about a little cup of coffee. *(As he continues toward his shop, they call again from inside: "Cards!")* I'm coming, I'm coming! *(He goes into his shop.)*

RIDOLFO: A fine business he runs, living off people's bad luck!

Act I

(Don Marzio enters.)

Here's a man who never stops talking—and according to him every word is gospel.

DON MARZIO: Coffee!

RIDOLFO: Coming right up.

DON MARZIO: What's new, Ridolfo? Any customers yet this morning?

RIDOLFO: It's still early in the day.

DON MARZIO: Early? It's past ten o'clock.

RIDOLFO: Oh no, sir, it's not eight yet.

DON MARZIO: You're joking.

RIDOLFO: No. I assure you it hasn't struck eight.

DON MARZIO: Oh get out, you ass. I counted the strokes of the town clock just now, and I tell you it's ten. Look at my watch. *(showing his watch)* It's never wrong.

RIDOLFO: It says ten minutes to eight.

DON MARZIO: It can't be. *(He takes out his lorgnette and looks at his watch.)*

RIDOLFO: What does it say?

DON MARZIO: It's wrong. It's ten o'clock. I just heard it strike.

RIDOLFO: Where did you buy your watch?

5

DON MARZIO: I ordered it from London.

RIDOLFO: Did they cheat you?

DON MARZIO: Nobody cheats me.

RIDOLFO: Either your watch is two hours off...

DON MARZIO: My watch is never off. It runs perfectly.

RIDOLFO: Then the time is ten to eight.

DON MARZIO: Don't be impudent. My watch is right, you're wrong, and if you don't look out I'll give you something to remember it by.

(Giovanni brings him coffee.)

RIDOLFO: Here's your coffee.

DON MARZIO: Have you seen anything of Eugenio?

RIDOLFO: Not yet.

DON MARZIO: *(drinking his coffee)* Probably at home cuddling his wife. What a soft character he is! Always with his darling wife!

RIDOLFO: Not last night. He was next door, gambling.

DON MARZIO: *(putting down his cup and rising)* That's what I said. Gambling, always gambling!

RIDOLFO: *(aside)* Always gambling! Always with his wife! Always with the devil—and not with you!

DON MARZIO: The other day he came to me, all secrecy, to borrow money on his wife's earrings.

RIDOLFO: Anybody can be short of cash. He trusted you not to tell.

DON MARZIO: I'm no blabber-mouth. I help everybody and never brag about it. *(showing the earrings in a jeweler's box)* Here they are— his wife's earrings. I lent him ten ducats on these; do you think I'm covered?

RIDOLFO: I'm no expert, but I imagine so.

DON MARZIO: Is your boy around? Hey, Trappola!

(Trappola comes from the shop.)

TRAPPOLA: You wanted me?

DON MARZIO: Go to the jeweler around the corner and show him these earrings. They belong to Eugenio's wife, you see. Tell him I'd like to know if they're worth the ten ducats I loaned on them.

TRAPPOLA: At your service. So—these belong to Signor Eugenio's wife?

DON MARZIO: Yes. He's stone broke.

RIDOLFO: Poor devil!

TRAPPOLA: Doesn't Signor Eugenio mind everybody knowing his private business?

DON MARZIO: I can keep a secret.

TRAPPOLA: I can't. I'm a blabber-mouth.

DON MARZIO: If you blab, people will stop trusting you.

TRAPPOLA: You told *me*.

DON MARZIO: Go see if the barber is ready to give me a shave!

TRAPPOLA: At your service. *(to Ridolfo)* For the price of a cup of coffee he expects an errand-boy too. *(He goes into the barber shop.)*

DON MARZIO: Ridolfo, how's that little dancer who lives around the corner?

RIDOLFO: I really don't know.

DON MARZIO: I hear that Count Leandro is keeping her.

RIDOLFO: Excuse me. The coffee is on the boil. *(He goes into his shop. Trappola returns from the barber shop.)*

TRAPPOLA: The barber has a customer under the hot towel, but as soon as he's done with that one, he'll be ready for you.

DON MARZIO: Tell me, do you know anything about the dancer around the corner?

TRAPPOLA: Lisaura? Well, I do and I don't.

DON MARZIO: Forget what you don't know and tell me what you do.

TRAPPOLA: You said people will stop trusting me if I blab.

DON MARZIO: You can tell me. Does Count Leandro frequent her flat? *(as Trappola ponders)* Is the Count a frequent visitor? *(as Trappola scratches his head)* Is Count Leandro with her often?

TRAPPOLA: Yes, he frequently frequents.

Act I

DON MARZIO: Oho!

TRAPPOLA: Sometimes.

DON MARZIO: What does sometimes mean?

TRAPPOLA: When nobody's looking.

DON MARZIO: Aha! He's trying to protect her reputation.

TRAPPOLA: He's trying to keep on her good side.

DON MARZIO: Oh, what a cunning Trappola you are! *(pinching his cheek)* Now go see about the earrings.

TRAPPOLA: Shall I tell the jeweler the earrings belong to Signor Eugenio's wife?

DON MARZIO: Yes, go ahead and tell him.

TRAPPOLA: You and I can certainly keep a secret! *(He leaves. Ridolfo comes from the coffee shop.)*

DON MARZIO: Ridolfo, if you really don't know anything about that little dancer, I can tell you a few things.

RIDOLFO: Frankly, I'm not much interested in other people's business.

DON MARZIO: You must be informed; how else can you deal with such people? She is kept by Leandro, the so-called Count. And to keep her—and keep himself in pocket money—he takes everything the poor girl earns. Because of him she's forced to do things she wouldn't do otherwise. He's her pimp!

RIDOLFO: I'm here all day long and I never see a soul go in her door but Count Leandro.

DON MARZIO: She has a back door! Traffic in and out all the time! She has a back door, you fool!

RIDOLFO: What if she does have a back door? I keep my nose out of it.

DON MARZIO: *(rising)* That's filthy. You talk to me like that?

RIDOLFO: I beg your pardon. Just a little joke.

DON MARZIO: Bring me a glass of rosolio.

RIDOLFO: I see my joke will cost me. *(He motions to Giovanni to serve Don Marzio his cordial.)*

DON MARZIO: This juicy bit about the little dancer is something to circulate.

RIDOLFO: Your rosolio.

DON MARZIO: *(drinking and musing)* In and out through the back door...a constant flow...flux and reflux...

RIDOLFO: That must make her miserable.

DON MARZIO: Eh?

RIDOLFO: All that flux through her back door.

(Eugenio, in evening clothes, comes from the gambling parlor, blinking bleary-eyed at the sky and stamping his feet.)

DON MARZIO: Your servant, Eugenio.

EUGENIO: What time is it?

DON MARZIO: Past ten o'clock.

RIDOLFO: And his watch is never wrong.

EUGENIO: Coffee!

RIDOLFO: Right away. *(He goes into his shop.)*

DON MARZIO: Well, my friend, how was your luck?

EUGENIO: *(ignoring Don Marzio)* Coffee!!

RIDOLFO: *(from inside)* It's on the way!

DON MARZIO: Did you lose?

EUGENIO: *(shouting)* Coffee!!!

DON MARZIO: I see. You lost everything. *(He sits as Pandolfo comes from his gambling den.)*

PANDOLFO: *(taking Eugenio aside)* Eugenio, a word with you.

EUGENIO: I know what you're going to say—I owe thirty ducats. I gave you my word I would pay.

PANDOLFO: The Count wants his winnings *now.* He's waiting.

(Don Marzio strains to hear what they are saying.)

RIDOLFO: *(to Eugenio)* Here's your coffee.

EUGENIO: *(to Ridolfo)* Go away! *(to Pandolfo)* He took me for a hundred in cash, so his night wasn't totally wasted.

PANDOLFO: What kind of sporting talk is that? You know the rules.

RIDOLFO: *(to Eugenio)* Your coffee's getting cold.

EUGENIO: Leave me alone!

RIDOLFO: If you don't want it…

EUGENIO: Get out of here!

RIDOLFO: *(retiring with the coffee)*…I'll drink it myself.

DON MARZIO: *(to Ridolfo)* What are they saying? *(Ridolfo does not answer.)*

EUGENIO: *(to Pandolfo)* I know the rules—but when there's no money, a man can't pay.

PANDOLFO: Listen, to save your hide, I might find thirty ducats for you.

EUGENIO: Good man! *(calling)* Coffee!

RIDOLFO: Now I'll have to make some fresh.

EUGENIO: I've been calling for coffee for an hour—and you haven't made it yet?

RIDOLFO: I brought you some and you told me to take it away.

PANDOLFO: *(to Eugenio)* You have to keep at him. Wheedle.

EUGENIO: *(to Ridolfo)* Listen, fix me a nice strong cup of coffee like a good fellow.

RIDOLFO: Of course. Right away. *(He goes into his shop.)*

DON MARZIO: Some big to-do. I'd love to know what it is.

Act I

EUGENIO: Look, Pandolfo, get me the thirty ducats however you can.

PANDOLFO: I have a friend who would lend the money, but he'll want some security—and interest, of course.

EUGENIO: I have plenty of security—my shop on the Rialto is full of fine cloth. I'll give him a lien on that and pay him when it's sold.

DON MARZIO: "I'll pay," he said. "I'll pay." So he did lose.

PANDOLFO: What about interest?

EUGENIO: I'll pay whatever seems fair.

PANDOLFO: I know he won't take less than a ducat a week.

EUGENIO: A ducat a week! That's usury!

RIDOLFO: *(to Eugenio)* Your coffee.

EUGENIO: *(to Ridolfo)* Get away from me!

RIDOLFO: Again?

EUGENIO: *(to Pandolfo)* A whole ducat a week?

PANDOLFO: On thirty ducats that's not much.

RIDOLFO: *(to Eugenio)* Do you want it or not?

EUGENIO: Get out of here or I'll throw it in your face!

RIDOLFO: Poor fellow, gambling has addled his wits. *(He takes the coffee back into the shop. Don Marzio rises and approaches Eugenio.)*

DON MARZIO: Is there some disagreement? Do you want me to arbitrate?

EUGENIO: It's nothing, Don Marzio. Just let me be.

DON MARZIO: If you need help, don't hesitate to say so. Pandolfo, what's the problem here?

PANDOLFO: A trifling matter we'd rather not announce to the whole world.

DON MARZIO: I'm a friend of Eugenio's, and he knows I never talk. I even lent him ten ducats on a pair of earrings—isn't that right?— and I never said a word to anyone.

EUGENIO: You don't have to say so now.

DON MARZIO: Oh, we can speak freely in front of Pandolfo. Have you lost a bit at gambling? Do you need a little money? I am at your service.

EUGENIO: To be honest with you, I owe thirty ducats.

DON MARZIO: Thirty ducats and the ten I already let you have makes forty. The earrings can't be worth that much.

PANDOLFO: I'll raise the thirty ducats for Eugenio. Leave it to me.

DON MARZIO: Oh good! Get forty. Then you can give me my ten and I'll turn the earrings over to you.

EUGENIO: Damn the day I ever got mixed up with this fellow!

DON MARZIO: *(to Eugenio)* Why don't you accept the money Pandolfo is offering you?

EUGENIO: Because he wants a ducat a week interest.

PANDOLFO: Not for myself. It's a friend who's lending the money.

EUGENIO: Speak to the Count; tell him to give me twenty-four hours to raise the money. I'm a man of honor; I'll pay.

PANDOLFO: He's going away and wants his money now.

EUGENIO: If I could sell a bolt or two of cloth, I could clear the debt.

PANDOLFO: Shall I see if I can find you a buyer?

EUGENIO: Would you do that for me? I'll pay you a commission.

PANDOLFO: Fine. Let me have a word with the Count and then I'm off. *(He goes into the gambling parlor.)*

DON MARZIO: *(to Eugenio)* Did you lose much?

EUGENIO: A hundred I had in cash and thirty more on credit.

DON MARZIO: You might have repaid me the ten you borrowed first.

(Pandolfo comes from his shop in hat and coat.)

PANDOLFO: The Count has fallen asleep with his head on the table. You stay here while I go raise this money for you.

EUGENIO: I'll be waiting.

PANDOLFO: *(aside)* This coat is wearing out. Now is my chance to get a new one free of charge. *(He leaves.)*

DON MARZIO: Sit down and let's have some coffee.

EUGENIO: *(calling as they sit)* Coffee!

(Ridolfo pokes his head from the shop.)

RIDOLFO: What's the game?

EUGENIO: Forgive me, Ridolfo. I'm frazzled today.

RIDOLFO: If you listened to your friends, you wouldn't get in these scrapes.

EUGENIO: What can I say? You're right.

RIDOLFO: I'll make you another coffee and we'll talk. *(He disappears into the shop.)*

DON MARZIO: Have you heard? The little dancer who plays so hard to get—she's kept by the Count.

EUGENIO: He can afford her, the way he wins at cards.

DON MARZIO: I've found out all about her. I know what time he goes to see her, what time he leaves…I know everything.

EUGENIO: And the Count is the only one she sees?

DON MARZIO: Don't be silly! She has a back door.

(Ridolfo enters with the coffee.)

RIDOLFO: *(to Eugenio)* This makes three coffees I've made for you.

DON MARZIO: Am I right, Ridolfo? About the dancer?

RIDOLFO: I told you—it's none of my business.

Act I

DON MARZIO: I get the lowdown on all these performers—the famous and the infamous, the virtuous and the virtuosi, the upright and the horizontal!

EUGENIO: Is this little dancer one of the horizontals?

DON MARZIO: Well, she has something to suit every taste. Am I right, Ridolfo?

RIDOLFO: I can tell you this—the whole neighborhood considers her a nice respectable girl.

DON MARZIO: Respectable? You call that little tart respectable?

RIDOLFO: I know for a fact nobody goes into her house.

DON MARZIO: By the back door! A steady flow in and out!

EUGENIO: She seems quiet and decent enough.

DON MARZIO: Decent? She's kept by the Count! And when he leaves, the back door is open to all comers.

EUGENIO: I tried, several times, and got nowhere with her. In fact, I never see anybody go in.

DON MARZIO: She has a secret door at the back. They go in that way.

EUGENIO: It could be.

DON MARZIO: It's a well known fact.

(The barber's apprentice comes from the barber shop.)

BARBER'S APPRENTICE: Don Marzio, if you want a shave, the barber is ready.

DON MARZIO: I'm coming. *(to Eugenio)* I'll tell you the rest after I have my shave. *(He goes into the barber shop, followed by the barber's apprentice.)*

EUGENIO: What do you think of that, Ridolfo? The little dancer!

RIDOLFO: Don't believe Don Marzio. You know how he talks.

EUGENIO: But he seems so sure.

RIDOLFO: *(pointing)* Look, there's the back door opening on the alley. From here you can see it plainly, and I swear nobody goes in that door.

EUGENIO: Except the Count?

RIDOLFO: Yes, the Count goes to see her. He's keeping her, but they say he intends to marry her.

EUGENIO: In that case, there's nothing wrong. But Don Marzio says anyone can get in.

RIDOLFO: I tell you no one does.

(Don Marzio comes from the barber shop with a white towel around his neck and lather on his face.)

DON MARZIO: And I tell you they go in by the back door!

BARBER'S APPRENTICE: Don Marzio, the water is getting cold.

DON MARZIO: By the back door! *(He re-enters the barber shop.)*

RIDOLFO: You see? Lather all over his face and he still won't shut up. He gossips about everybody. How did you get mixed up with him? Couldn't you have borrowed ten ducats from somebody else?

EUGENIO: So you know about that too.

RIDOLFO: He crowed about it to everybody in the street.

EUGENIO: You know how it is—in a pinch a man grasps at straws.

RIDOLFO: And just now you grasped at the flimsiest straw in sight.

EUGENIO: Pandolfo? You think he means to cheat me? *(as Ridolfo shrugs)* Where else can I turn? I have to come up with thirty ducats to save my honor. I'd like to pay Don Marzio his ten ducats, to stop him pestering me; and there are a couple of other little debts coming due. If I could sell a few bolts of cloth, I could settle them all.

RIDOLFO: What kind of cloth is it?

EUGENIO: Paduan wool, worth fourteen lire a yard.

RIDOLFO: Would you like me to sell it for you at a fair price?

EUGENIO: I'd be eternally grateful.

RIDOLFO: I'll need a little time.

EUGENIO: Time? He's expecting his thirty ducats today!

RIDOLFO: All right, you make out an order consigning me two bolts of cloth and I'll lend you the thirty ducats myself.

EUGENIO: I'll find some way to repay you.

RIDOLFO: Please—this is something I owe to the memory of your father. He helped me set up this shop, and I can't stand by now and watch these dogs rip you to pieces.

EUGENIO: Ridolfo, you are a real friend.

RIDOLFO: Just draw up the consignment. It should be in writing.

EUGENIO: I'm ready. You dictate and I'll write.

RIDOLFO: What's the name of your chief clerk?

EUGENIO: Pasquino de' Cavoli.

(Ridolfo dictates and Eugenio writes.)

RIDOLFO: "Pasquino de' Cavoli...please consign to Ridolfo Gamboni...two bolts of Paduan cloth...to be sold by him for my account...in return for freely lending me, without interest...the sum of thirty ducats." Sign and date it.

EUGENIO: There.

RIDOLFO: Do you trust me?

EUGENIO: I should hope so!

RIDOLFO: And I trust you. *(counting out the money)* Here are thirty ducats.

EUGENIO: Old friend, I'm much obliged.

RIDOLFO: Signor Eugenio, I give you this money so you can meet your obligations. Only allow me to say this, for the sake of old times— forget the gambling and the shady cronies. Tend to your business and your wife, and use your common sense. *(He goes into his shop.)*

Act I

EUGENIO: He's not far wrong, I have to admit. My wife must have worried herself sick last night. Women do, when their men don't come home. They imagine a thousand disasters—I was with another woman, or I fell into the canal, or I skipped town because of the debts... I know she loves me; it's all she thinks about. I love her too, but I like my freedom. Still, I see that if I did things her way, life would be smoother. I'll have to turn over a new leaf... How many times have I said those words? *(He sees Lisaura at her window.)* Look at that. Such grand airs! There may really be a little door with a secret latch. *(to Lisaura)* Lady! My humble respects.

LISAURA: Your servant.

EUGENIO: Have you been up long? Have you had your coffee?

LISAURA: Not yet.

EUGENIO: May I send some up for you?

LISAURA: Thank you; don't trouble.

EUGENIO: No trouble at all. Boys, take this lady some coffee.

LISAURA: I drink chocolate.

EUGENIO: Chocolate then, or whatever she likes. I'll pay.

LISAURA: Thank you again, but I make my own.

EUGENIO: Good stuff, I'll bet. Would you like me to help you stir up a pot?

LISAURA: You mustn't put yourself out.

EUGENIO: Just say the word and I'll pop up and share a little with you. Come on, open up. We'll get acquainted.

LISAURA: You must pardon me if I don't open up so easily.

EUGENIO: Hey, what about the back door?

LISAURA: My visitors come to the front door. Tell me, have you seen Count Leandro?

EUGENIO: I only wish I hadn't.

LISAURA: You gambled with him last night?

EUGENIO: Yes, I did—worse luck. But why are we talking where everybody can hear us? I'll come up and tell you all about it.

LISAURA: I told you—I open to no one.

EUGENIO: You need permission from the Count? I'll call him. He's in the gambling house—asleep.

LISAURA: Then let him sleep.

(Count Leandro comes from the gambling parlor.)

LEANDRO: I'm not asleep; I'm admiring this gentleman's audacity.

EUGENIO: What about the lady's audacity? She won't let me in.

LEANDRO: What did you expect?

EUGENIO: According to Don Marzio—some flux and reflux, some in and out.

LEANDRO: Don Marzio is a liar.

EUGENIO: That may be, but couldn't you introduce me to the lady? I'd like to pay my respects.

Act I

LEANDRO: You'd do better to pay me my thirty ducats.

EUGENIO: You'll get your money. The loser has twenty-four hours to cover his debts.

LEANDRO: Look at this seedy merchant, Lisaura. He's broke and still wants to play the carefree Lothario.

EUGENIO: Not as broke as you think. Here, take your thirty ducats and stop making foolish noises. *(He hands Leandro the money he got from Ridolfo and goes to the coffee shop and sits.)*

LEANDRO: As long as he pays, let him talk. Open up.

LISAURA: Where have you been all night?

LEANDRO: Open the door!

LISAURA: Go to the devil!

(Leandro pours coins into his hat and shows them to Lisaura.)

LEANDRO: Open!

LISAURA: This once I will. *(She disappears from the window to open the door.)*

LEANDRO: She likes the sound of money. *(The door opens and he goes inside.)*

EUGENIO: He gets in and I don't? She needs a few lessons.

(Placida enters dressed as a pilgrim.)

PLACIDA: Alms...Alms for a poor pilgrim. *(to Eugenio)* Give a little something to the needy, and heaven bless you.

EUGENIO: What's this pilgrim get-up? Fun? Or a confidence game?

PLACIDA: Neither one.

EUGENIO: Then why do you go around like this?

PLACIDA: Out of need.

EUGENIO: Need of what?

PLACIDA: Everything.

EUGENIO: Does that include company?

PLACIDA: I'd have no need of company if my husband had not deserted me.

EUGENIO: It's the same old song—my husband deserted me. Where are you from?

PLACIDA: Torino.

EUGENIO: Your husband too? What was his business there?

PLACIDA: He was clerk to a merchant, but he didn't like work.

EUGENIO: I've had a touch of that ailment. Still have.

PLACIDA: Please help me. I just arrived in Venice, looking for him.

EUGENIO: What's his name?

PLACIDA: Flaminio Ardenti.

EUGENIO: Never heard of him.

Act I

PLACIDA: He may have changed his name.

EUGENIO: Look around; you might find him—if he's here.

PLACIDA: He'll run if he sees me.

EUGENIO: It's carnival time—wear a mask. That way you can catch him unawares.

PLACIDA: How? I have no place to stay, no money, nothing...

EUGENIO: The ways things are going, I may turn pilgrim myself. Look, this inn is quite respectable.

PLACIDA: I can't go to an inn without paying.

EUGENIO: My pretty little pilgrim, if half a ducat will do you any good, here it is. That cleans me out completely.

PLACIDA: Thank you; I'm truly grateful. But more than half a ducat— more than any amount of money—I'd appreciate your protection.

EUGENIO: *(aside)* Aha. Doesn't want half a ducat. Wants more.

(Don Marzio comes from the barber shop. Looking at the pilgrim through his lorgnette, he goes to sit at the coffee shop.)

DON MARZIO: Eugenio with a pilgrim! That's interesting.

PLACIDA: If you would kindly introduce me at the inn, the host won't take me for a vagrant and chase me away.

EUGENIO: All right. I'll go in with you. The host knows me.

DON MARZIO: I think I've seen her before.

EUGENIO: If you don't find your husband, come to me and we'll see what else we can do.

DON MARZIO: I'd like to hear what they're saying.

PLACIDA: Your kindness is a great comfort. But the attentions of a young man like you to a woman like me might be misunderstood.

EUGENIO: If we stopped to think about that, no good would ever get done. Anyhow, gossips will always find something to drool over. It makes them look good in comparison.

PLACIDA: You have a kind heart.

DON MARZIO: *(to Eugenio)* My friend, who is this lovely pilgrim?

EUGENIO: *(ignoring Don Marzio, to Placida)* Shall we go to the inn?

PLACIDA: You lead the way.

(Eugenio leads her into the inn.)

DON MARZIO: That Eugenio never misses a trick—not even a pilgrim. She looks like the one who went from table to table begging at the carnival last year. I never gave her anything, I can tell you.—Boys, isn't Trappola back yet with the earrings Eugenio gave me for a loan of ten ducats?

EUGENIO: *(reappearing from the inn)* What are you saying about me?

DON MARZIO: There you are! Back so soon? You've picked up a pilgrim!

EUGENIO: She's looking for a place to stay. Can't a man help somebody in need?

DON MARZIO: Oh, that's commendable! Poor thing, hasn't she found anybody since last year?

EUGENIO: What do you mean? You know this pilgrim?

DON MARZIO: I should think I do! She was here for the last carnival, cadging from the customers.

EUGENIO: She says she's never been in Venice before.

DON MARZIO: And you believe her? My poor boy!

EUGENIO: Where was she from, the one last year?

DON MARZIO: Milan.

EUGENIO: This one is from Torino.

DON MARZIO: Oh, that's right. It was Torino.

EUGENIO: She's the wife of a man named Flaminio Ardenti.

DON MARZIO: Yes, she had someone who passed for her husband last year too.

EUGENIO: This one's husband left her.

DON MARZIO: The way they live! They change husbands twice a month.

EUGENIO: How can you be sure it's the same woman?

DON MARZIO: My lorgnette is never wrong. Besides, I recognize her voice.

EUGENIO: What was the name of the one you saw last year?

DON MARZIO: The name? Oh, I don't recall.

EUGENIO: This one is named Placida.

DON MARZIO: That was it—Placida.

EUGENIO: Are you sure? This poor woman needs a place to stay.

DON MARZIO: Believe me, this pilgrim of yours is not looking for a vacancy; she's got one to offer.

EUGENIO: Wait here; I'll be back. I intend to know the truth about this. *(He goes into the inn.)*

DON MARZIO: She's the one, definitely. I didn't get a good look at her face, but she's the one. When she saw me, she hid in the inn.

(Vittoria has come in, masked.)

VITTORIA: *(taking off her mask)* Don Marzio, your servant.

DON MARZIO: Oh, a masker! I'm your slave.

VITTORIA: Have you seen my husband by any chance?

DON MARZIO: Yes, I have. *(taking her aside)* He's in the inn with a little pilgrim in long curls.

VITTORIA: How long has he been there?

DON MARZIO: Only a minute or two. This pretty pilgrim happened along and struck his fancy and he took her straight into the inn.

VITTORIA: The rash fool! He'll destroy his reputation completely!

DON MARZIO: You must have waited up for him quite a while last night.

Act I

VITTORIA: I was terrified that something awful had happened to him.

DON MARZIO: Like losing a hundred in cash and another thirty on credit?

VITTORIA: He lost all that money?

DON MARZIO: Oh yes, and more besides, gambling all day and all night like a wild man. Now he has only to sell what little cloth he has in stock and he's done for. He has pawned everything he owns.

VITTORIA: That's not true!

DON MARZIO: You doubt my word?

VITTORIA: I ought to know better than you.

DON MARZIO: He even borrowed from me on a pair of…well, I'll not say any more.

VITTORIA: Borrowed on what? Something I don't know about?

DON MARZIO: Oh, you have a model husband!

VITTORIA: You won't tell me what it was?

DON MARZIO: I'm a man of honor. I'll not tell.

(Trappola comes in with the jeweler's box containing the earrings.)

TRAPPOLA: Here I am. The jeweler said…*(softly to Don Marzio)* Ooooh! Signor Eugenio's wife! She mustn't hear this.

DON MARZIO: *(softly to Trappola)* Well, what did the jeweler say?

TRAPPOLA: *(softly)* He says they probably cost more than ten ducats but he wouldn't give that much for them.

DON MARZIO: Then I'm not covered? *(to Vittoria)* You see the tricks your husband plays? He leaves me these earrings as security for ten ducats and they're not worth six.

VITTORIA: Those are my earrings! They cost more than thirty.

DON MARZIO: Thirty what—pebbles?

VITTORIA: Will you hold them till tomorrow? I'll get ten ducats for you.

DON MARZIO: You're in cahoots with him. Don't try to bamboozle me. I intend to show them to all the jewelers in Venice.

VITTORIA: Don't say they're mine! Consider my reputation!

DON MARZIO: Talk to the man who borrowed my ten ducats—which I want back! *(He leaves.)*

VITTORIA: What a rude man! Trappola, did my husband gamble all night?

TRAPPOLA: Well, let me put it this way—this morning he was still sitting exactly where I saw him last night.

VITTORIA: That rotten vice! And now he's cavorting with a strange woman?

TRAPPOLA: Probably. I've seen him buzzing around her often enough.

VITTORIA: They say she just came to town.

TRAPPOLA: Oh no, she's been here for months.

Act I

VITTORIA: Isn't she a pilgrim?

TRAPPOLA: No, she's a dancer.

VITTORIA: And she's staying here at the inn?

TRAPPOLA: No. There's her place. *(He points to Lisaura's window.)*

VITTORIA: There? But Don Marzio said Eugenio is at the inn with a pilgrim.

TRAPPOLA: Oh really? He's got a pilgrim too?

VITTORIA: There's another woman? One here and one there?

TRAPPOLA: Larboard, starboard, swivel and tack—he likes to keep the wind at his back.

VITTORIA: How long must I stand for this? I'll take him to court.

TRAPPOLA: You're absolutely right. Here he comes from the inn.

VITTORIA: Leave me alone with him. I'll surprise him. *(She puts on her mask.)*

TRAPPOLA: Whatever you say. *(He leaves. Eugenio re-enters.)*

EUGENIO: I don't know which one to believe. Of course Don Marzio is a liar and a gossip; but who can trust these wandering beggars either?—Aha! A lady in a mask! Will you have some coffee? Or maybe something else? Just say the word.

VITTORIA: I don't need coffee. I need bread. *(She unmasks.)*

EUGENIO: What is this? What are you doing here?

VITTORIA: I'm here because I'm desperate.

EUGENIO: What do you mean—wearing a mask so early in the morning!

VITTORIA: Fun, isn't it—so early in the morning?

EUGENIO: Go home! Go home this minute!

VITTORIA: I go home while you stay here and frolic? A fine life you lead, my husband!

EUGENIO: Enough back-talk! Go home, if you know what's good for you!

VITTORIA: I'll go. I'll go to my father's. He'll see I get justice—and my dowry back.

EUGENIO: Is that all you care about me?

VITTORIA: You're destroying my love for you.

EUGENIO: What have I done?

VITTORIA: You stay out all night! Gambling!

EUGENIO: Who said I was gambling?

VITTORIA: Don Marzio. You lost a hundred ducats, he said, and thirty more on credit.

EUGENIO: You believe that man?

VITTORIA: And you've been playing around with some pilgrim.

EUGENIO: Who said so?

Act I

VITTORIA: Don Marzio.

EUGENIO: Damn him! It's not true!

VITTORIA: And pawning my earrings without telling me. Is that the way to treat a wife who tries so hard to keep you decent? Look at me!

EUGENIO: How did you know about the earrings?

VITTORIA: Don Marzio told me.

EUGENIO: I'll put his tongue in a clamp!

VITTORIA: Don Marzio says—everybody says!—you'll be completely ruined. And before that happens I want my dowry back.

EUGENIO: Vittoria, if you loved me you wouldn't talk like that.

VITTORIA: That's been my problem—loving you too much.

EUGENIO: You're going home to your father? You don't want to stay with me any more?

VITTORIA: Not till you grow up and show some sense.

EUGENIO: *(getting angry)* Don't preach at me!

VITTORIA: Hush! You want people to hear?

EUGENIO: If you were so proper you wouldn't come to a coffee shop and harangue your husband.

VITTORIA: Don't worry. This is the last you'll see of me.

EUGENIO: Go on! Get out of here!

VITTORIA: I'm going. I obey like a good wife—even when my husband is a brute and a fool. Some day you'll wish you had me back. When you're writhing in anguish, you'll whimper for the loving little wife who helped you out of your miserable scrapes. But you won't have me to abuse any more. I'll be far away from you and your betrayals. I may suffer and weep for love of you, but I'll never lay eyes on your deceitful face again. *(She leaves.)*

EUGENIO: If she takes back her dowry, I'm done for. Oh, she'd never do that! She talks but she'll never actually do it. Poor old girl, I'll go home and jolly her up a little. All she wants is a good cuddle.

ACT II

Scene: The same.

At rise: Ridolfo enters from the street.

RIDOLFO: Hey! Boys!

(Trappola comes from inside the coffee shop.)

What's this? Nobody minding the shop?

TRAPPOLA: I kept an eye peeled and an ear cocked from inside. Besides, what could anybody steal?

RIDOLFO: Cups! People steal coffee cups from us poor shopkeepers.

TRAPPOLA: So that's why they eat out—to stock up on crockery!

RIDOLFO: Where is Signor Eugenio? Has he gone?

TRAPPOLA: You should have been here! His wife came looking for him. Tears, sobs, lamentations! He's unfaithful, he's cruel! She worked him over—first all loving, then jeering at him—until she ground him into meal.

RIDOLFO: Where did he go?

TRAPPOLA: Need you ask? A man's out all night, his wife hunts him down, and you ask where he goes? He slinks back home, that's where.

RIDOLFO: He didn't leave any word for me?

TRAPPOLA: He came to the door to say he was counting on you to sell that cloth. It's his only hope, he says.

RIDOLFO: I did sell it—two bolts at thirteen lire a yard. I've got the money, but he mustn't know. If I give him all of it at once, he'll spend it before the day's out.

TRAPPOLA: He'll want the whole bundle.

RIDOLFO: I won't tell him. I'll parcel it out to him bit by bit.

TRAPPOLA: Here he comes: *forte dux in aero.*

RIDOLFO: Hey, isn't that Latin? What's it mean?

TRAPPOLA: Forty ducks in a row. (*Grinning, he retires into the shop.*)

RIDOLFO: He's a funny fellow—speaks Latin but doesn't know you can't *get* forty ducks in a row; they won't cooperate.

(*Enter Eugenio.*)

EUGENIO: Well, Ridolfo old friend, my clerk tells me you picked up the two bolts of cloth. Did you sell them?

RIDOLFO: I managed to.

EUGENIO: For how much?

RIDOLFO: Thirteen lire a yard.

EUGENIO: Good! Ready money?

RIDOLFO: Partly. The rest on time.

EUGENIO: Uh-oh… How much cash?

RIDOLFO: Forty ducats.

EUGENIO: That's not too bad. Let me have the money. It saves my hide.

RIDOLFO: Easy now, Signor Eugenio. I already lent you thirty ducats.

EUGENIO: I'll repay you when you collect the balance.

RIDOLFO: Forgive me, but that's not exactly honorable. I did this as a favor, and now you want me to wait for my money? I have expenses too, you know.

EUGENIO: You're right. Keep thirty ducats for yourself and give me the other ten.

RIDOLFO: Aren't you going to pay off Don Marzio?

EUGENIO: He's got the earrings. He'll wait for his ten ducats.

RIDOLFO: Do you want him gossiping about you? Bragging about all he lent you?

EUGENIO: If I repay him, what will I do for ready money?

RIDOLFO: How much do you actually need?

EUGENIO: Oh—ten or twelve ducats.

RIDOLFO: Here's ten. And this ten here I'll give to Don Marzio, to redeem those earrings.

EUGENIO: When do I get the balance of the money for the cloth you sold?

RIDOLFO: I'll collect it for you, don't you worry. Meanwhile, spend only what you really have to.

EUGENIO: Right. I'm obliged to you, my friend. Don't forget to keep a percentage for yourself, as a commission.

RIDOLFO: I'm surprised at you! I run a coffee shop, not a brokerage. If I help a friend, I don't expect a commission. *(He goes into his shop.)*

EUGENIO: Now there's a worthy man! For someone who runs a coffee shop he does preach a lot. But at least he's got good sense. I wish I had some of it.

(Count Leandro comes from Lisaura's.)

LEANDRO: Eugenio, here's the money you lost last night, all of it in this purse. Like to win it back? I'll play you for it.

EUGENIO: I've given up gambling. I have no luck.

LEANDRO: Luck can change. It may be your turn next.

EUGENIO: It's never my turn; it's always yours.

LEANDRO: *(yawning)* I'm so sleepy I probably couldn't hang on to the cards, but I'll play you a hand or two. If you're out of cash, I'll trust you.

EUGENIO: *(showing his purse)* I've got money. I just don't want to play.

LEANDRO: Match you for a cup of chocolate anyhow.

EUGENIO: No, I'm not in the mood.

LEANDRO: Come on—a cup of chocolate. Be a sport.

EUGENIO: I tell you...

Act II

LEANDRO: One chocolate, that's all! And the first to suggest a serious game forfeits a ducat.

EUGENIO: All right, just for a cup of chocolate.

LEANDRO: *(to himself)* Got him! He's in the bag!

(He and Eugenio go into the gambling parlor. Enter Don Marzio.)

DON MARZIO: All the jewelers agree these earrings are not worth ten ducats. I'll never help anybody out again if they're dying at my feet.

(Enter Ridolfo from the coffee shop.)

Where the devil is Eugenio? These precious earrings aren't worth a thing! Eugenio cheated me, the swindler! He's run away to keep from paying me!

RIDOLFO: Here, Don Marzio—here are ten ducats. Give me the earrings.

DON MARZIO: *(examining the coins through his lorgnette)* They're not counterfeit, are they?

RIDOLFO: I guarantee them. If anything's wrong, you can come to me.

DON MARZIO: You're paying out of your own pocket?

RIDOLFO: This is Signor Eugenio's money.

DON MARZIO: Where did he get it? Did he win at cards?

RIDOLFO: I don't know.

DON MARZIO: No, he must have sold some cloth, through Pandolfo. Did Pandolfo give you the money?

RIDOLFO: Do you want to be paid or not?

DON MARZIO: Give it here. Probably sold his cloth for next to nothing.

RIDOLFO: Do I get the earrings?

DON MARZIO: You're taking them to him?

RIDOLFO: That's right.

DON MARZIO: To Eugenio himself? Or to his wife?

RIDOLFO: *(losing patience)* One or the other—what does it matter?

DON MARZIO: Where is he?

RIDOLFO: I've no idea.

DON MARZIO: Then you'll have to take them to his wife, won't you? I'll go with you.

RIDOLFO: Give them here. You can trust me.

DON MARZIO: *(starting off)* Come on, we'll go to his wife together.

RIDOLFO: I know the way. I don't need your help.

DON MARZIO: I want to do her this courtesy myself. Come along, come along. *(He leaves.)*

RIDOLFO: Boys, mind the shop. *(He follows Don Marzio off. The waiters are at the coffee shop as Eugenio comes from the gambling parlor.)*

Act II

EUGENIO: What cursed luck! I lose all my money—for a cup of chocolate! Ten ducats! But the way he did it, that's what hurts! Dragging me in there, winning all I had, and then refusing me credit! Now, when I'm hot—and ready to play till dawn! Let Ridolfo say what he likes, he has to advance me some more money. Boys, where's your boss?

GIOVANNI: He just left.

EUGENIO: Where did he go?

GIOVANNI: I don't know.

EUGENIO: Damn Ridolfo anyway! Where the devil is he when I need him? *(calling into the door of the gambling parlor)* Count, wait just a minute! I'll be right back! *(about to leave)* I want to see if I can find that damned Ridolfo.

(Pandolfo comes from the street.)

PANDOLFO: Where are you off to in such a hurry?

EUGENIO: Have you seen Ridolfo?

PANDOLFO: Me? No.

EUGENIO: How about my bolts of wool—have you sold them?

PANDOLFO: Yes, I've made a good deal for you.

EUGENIO: Fine! How much?

PANDOLFO: It wasn't easy. I showed it to more than ten prospects, and nobody thought it was worth a bid.

EUGENIO: This buyer you finally found—how much will he pay?

PANDOLFO: I talked him into giving me eight lire a yard.

EUGENIO: What! Ridolfo got me thirteen!

PANDOLFO: Cash?

EUGENIO: Partly. The rest on time.

PANDOLFO: On time! I could have got *sixteen* on time! I'm getting you cash; you'd better grab it.

EUGENIO: That cloth cost me ten lire wholesale!

PANDOLFO: What's a loss of two lire when you're getting ready money?

EUGENIO: Can't you haggle with him a little? So I break even at least.

PANDOLFO: Not a hope. He won't budge.

EUGENIO: I'll have to settle for that then. Make the deal.

PANDOLFO: Write me an order for the two bolts of wool and I'll bring you your money in half an hour.

EUGENIO: All right. Boys, give me a pen and paper.

(The waiters bring writing materials and set them on one of the tables.)

PANDOLFO: Write your clerk to give me the two bolts of wool I pointed out.

EUGENIO: Whichever you want—it's all the same to me. *(Eugenio begins to write.)*

PANDOLFO: *(to himself)* I'll get a fine new coat out of this!

Act II

(Ridolfo comes from the street.)

RIDOLFO: Business, Signor Eugenio? More business?

EUGENIO: *(writing)* This order's for cash. I need ready money, so I have to sell two more bolts of cloth, below cost— at a sacrifice.

PANDOLFO: I wouldn't call it a sacrifice. You're selling at the best price you're bid.

RIDOLFO: What are they giving you a yard?

EUGENIO: I'm ashamed to tell you. Eight lire.

PANDOLFO: But cash in hand! Ready cash!

RIDOLFO: Why rush into a deal at such a miserable price?

EUGENIO: I need the money.

PANDOLFO: It's not easy to get cash at short notice.

RIDOLFO: *(to Eugenio)* How much do you actually need? Six or seven ducats?

EUGENIO: *(resuming writing)* Get out! I need real money.

RIDOLFO: Wait. How much will you get for two bolts at eight lire a yard?

EUGENIO: Let's see—sixty yards in a bolt...two bolts—a hundred and twenty yards...A hundred and twenty times...

PANDOLFO: Minus the commission.

RIDOLFO: Whose commission?

PANDOLFO: Mine! Mine!

RIDOLFO: I see. A hundred and twenty yards at eight lire—how many ducats does that make?

EUGENIO: Well, four for every eleven...Ten times eleven is a hundred and ten, plus eleven is a hundred twenty-one. Four times eleven, forty-four. Forty-four ducats minus one—that's forty-three ducats and fourteen lire.

PANDOLFO: Call it an even forty, to round off for the commission.

EUGENIO: Over three ducats for commission?

PANDOLFO: Of course! You're getting cash, remember.

EUGENIO: All right, all right.

RIDOLFO: What a chiseler! Now how much does it come to at *thirteen* lire?

EUGENIO: Oh, a lot more, naturally.

PANDOLFO: But that's on time! He won't get cash!

RIDOLFO: Figure it up.

EUGENIO: I'll do it on paper. A hundred and twenty yards at thirteen lire a yard...Three times zero; two times three is six; one times three; one times zero; one times one. Adds up to: zero; six; two and three are five; one. One thousand five hundred and sixty lire.

RIDOLFO: How many ducats does that make?

EUGENIO: Just a second. *(counting)* Seventy ducats and twenty lire.

RIDOLFO: And that's without commission.

EUGENIO: Without commission.

PANDOLFO: But how long do you have to wait for your money? A bird in the hand...

RIDOLFO: From me you have already had thirty ducats to begin with, then ten, which makes forty; and ten for the earrings I got back for you—that makes fifty. So far you've had from me ten ducats more—in cash—than he's about to give you, this wonderful man with his commission.

PANDOLFO: And you can go rot in hell!

EUGENIO: *(to Ridolfo)* But I need money—now.

RIDOLFO: You need money? Here you are—twenty ducats and twenty lire, the balance from seventy ducats, twenty lire—without paying any commission at all—cash in hand, no cheating, no gouging, no swindling.

EUGENIO: In that case, Ridolfo my friend, I thank you. I'm evermore beholden to you. I'll tear this order up. *(to Pandolfo)* And I have no further need of you and your commissions.

PANDOLFO: The devil brought him here and sent my new coat up in smoke. *(to Eugenio)* All right. I was just doing you a favor. You might at least offer me a drink after all my trouble.

EUGENIO: Wait. *(taking a coin from the purse Ridolfo has given him)* Here's a ducat.

PANDOLFO: Much obliged. *(to himself)* I'll get even another time.

RIDOLFO: *(looking anxiously at Eugenio)* There he goes, throwing his money away already.

PANDOLFO: *(to Eugenio)* Anything else I can do for you?

EUGENIO: No hard feelings?

PANDOLFO: *(miming card-playing behind Ridolfo's back)* Would you like…?

EUGENIO: *(softly)* I'll be along in a minute.

PANDOLFO: He'll gamble it away before dinner. He'd rather play cards than eat. *(He goes into his gambling parlor.)*

EUGENIO: What happened, Ridolfo? Did your buyer pay off the balance early?

RIDOLFO: To tell you the truth, I had the money in my pocket, but I didn't want to give it all to you for fear you'd squander it.

EUGENIO: I'm not a child!—Well, forget it. Where are the earrings?

RIDOLFO: I delivered them to your wife. Don Marzio insisted on going along.

EUGENIO: Did you talk to her? What did she say? How did she sound?

RIDOLFO: She does nothing but cry, poor woman. Breaks your heart.

EUGENIO: If you'd seen how mad she was at me! Wanted to go home to her father! Wanted her dowry back!

RIDOLFO: How did you get around her?

EUGENIO: With a few sweet words and a hug or two.

Act II

RIDOLFO: It's easy to see she adores you. She has a loving nature.

EUGENIO: But when she's mad, she's wild.

RIDOLFO: Then don't mistreat her. She's a lady and gently brought up. She asked me to tell you to be home in time for dinner.

EUGENIO: Yes, yes, I'm going now.

(Pandolfo comes from the gambling parlor, hawks and spits, obviously to get Eugenio's attention. Pandolfo signals that Leandro is waiting to start a game of cards; Eugenio indicates he'll be right there. Pandolfo goes back inside. Ridolfo has seen none of this.)

RIDOLFO: It's nearly dinner time. Go comfort her.

EUGENIO: Yes, right away. I'll see you later.

RIDOLFO: Anything I can do for you, just let me know.

EUGENIO: I'm much obliged to you. *(He would like to go gamble but is afraid that Ridolfo will see him.)*

RIDOLFO: Anything more you need?

EUGENIO: Nothing. Not a thing. See you later.

RIDOLFO: Your servant then. *(He turns toward his shop. Eugenio, seeing that Ridolfo is not watching, slips into the gambling parlor.)* You might ask why bother about a young man who's no kin to you. Well, can't a man help out a family that's done so much for him?

(Enter Don Marzio.)

DON MARZIO: What an ass! What a stupid ass!

RIDOLFO: Who is it now, Don Marzio?

DON MARZIO: Listen, Ridolfo—you want a good laugh? Some asinine doctor claims that warm water is better for you than cold.

RIDOLFO: You don't agree?

DON MARZIO: Hot water weakens the stomach.

RIDOLFO: It certainly relaxes the tissues.

DON MARZIO: What tissues?

RIDOLFO: In our stomach we have muscles—or something like that— to grind up our food; and when they go slack, we get indigestion.

DON MARZIO: No, no, no! Hot water relaxes the *ventricle!* That prevents the systolic and the diastolic...

RIDOLFO: Ventricle?

DON MARZIO: Yes, the cavity.

RIDOLFO: What cavity?

DON MARZIO: The stomach, you fool! Then the systolic and the diastolic...

RIDOLFO: The systolic and the diastolic? What are they?

DON MARZIO: You donkey! The systolic and the diastolic are the two tissues that grind up your digestion!

RIDOLFO: *(aside)* He's all mixed up. Worse than Trappola.

(Lisaura appears at her window.)

Act II

DON MARZIO: *(to Ridolfo)* Hey! Our little friend with the back door!

RIDOLFO: Excuse me. I've got to tend to the coffee. *(He goes into his shop.)*

DON MARZIO: The lazy fool probably wants to close up shop early. *(to Lisaura, ogling her through his lorgnette)* Your servant, lady.

LISAURA: Your very humble servant.

DON MARZIO: How are you?

LISAURA: Well enough, thank you.

DON MARZIO: Have you seen Count Leandro? The Count is a friend of mine.

LISAURA: Delighted to hear it.

DON MARZIO: What a fine gentleman he is!

LISAURA: You're very kind.

DON MARZIO: Listen, is he your husband?

LISAURA: I never discuss my private affairs in public.

DON MARZIO: Open your door then and we'll talk inside.

LISAURA: You must excuse me. I'm not receiving visitors.

DON MARZIO: Go on!

LISAURA: No. Really.

DON MARZIO: I'll come to the back.

LISAURA: You have fantasies about a back door too, do you?

DON MARZIO: Don't pretend with me. I know very well you bring people in through the back.

LISAURA: I'm a respectable woman.

DON MARZIO: *(reaching into his pocket)* Would you like some dried chestnuts?

LISAURA: No, thank you very much.

DON MARZIO: They're very good, you know. I toast them myself, on my estate.

LISAURA: You're quite a toaster, I see. Well, you burn me to a crisp.

DON MARZIO: Very witty! If you can turn as quick a trick…on your feet, you're quite a…dancer.

LISAURA: That's none of your business.

DON MARZIO: Oh, pooh.

(Placida, in her pilgrim garb, appears at the window of the inn.)

PLACIDA: *(to herself)* I don't see Eugenio anywhere.

DON MARZIO: *(to Lisaura, viewing Placida through his lorgnette)* Say! Notice the pilgrim?

LISAURA: Who is she?

DON MARZIO: A good-time girl.

LISAURA: Does the innkeeper take in people like that?

Act II

DON MARZIO: She has a protector—know what I mean? She's kept.

LISAURA: Who keeps her?

DON MARZIO: Eugenio.

LISAURA: And him a married man? Well!

DON MARZIO: She was here last year too, making the rounds.

LISAURA: *(closing her window and withdrawing)* Your servant, then. I'll not be seen with a woman of that sort.

DON MARZIO: Ho, ho, ho! That's rich! Our little dancer retires for fear of ruining her reputation! *(staring through his lorgnette at Placida)* Lady pilgrim, my respects.

PLACIDA: Your devoted servant.

DON MARZIO: Where is Eugenio?

PLACIDA: You know Signor Eugenio?

DON MARZIO: Oh, we're the best of friends. I've just been to see his wife.

PLACIDA: You mean Signor Eugenio is married?

DON MARZIO: Of course. But that doesn't keep him from cavorting around. Did you see that lady at the window?

PLACIDA: I saw her, yes. She politely shut her window in my face.

DON MARZIO: She calls herself a dancer, but—! You get my meaning.

PLACIDA: She's one of those, is she?

DON MARZIO: Yes, and Eugenio is one of her customers.

PLACIDA: But he's married!

DON MARZIO: And to a beautiful wife, I must say.

PLACIDA: Well, there are young libertines everywhere.

DON MARZIO: Did he lead you to believe he wasn't married?

PLACIDA: It's nothing to me whether he is or he isn't.

DON MARZIO: You don't mind, eh? You take him as he is.

PLACIDA: It makes no difference in my relationship with him.

DON MARZIO: Oh, I know! With you it's one man today, another tomorrow.

PLACIDA: What do you mean by that? Explain yourself.

DON MARZIO: *(reaching into his pocket)* Would you like a couple of dried chestnuts?

PLACIDA: No, thank you.

DON MARZIO: I'll gladly give you some.

PLACIDA: You're too generous.

DON MARZIO: Actually, for someone as attractive as you, a few chestnuts aren't much. If you insist, I'll add a couple of lire.

PLACIDA: Boorish beast! *(She closes the window and disappears.)*

DON MARZIO: She won't stoop to two lire, but last year she was glad to take a lot less. *(calling loudly)* Ridolfo?

(Enter Ridolfo.)

RIDOLFO: You called?

DON MARZIO: Women must be in short supply. They turn up their noses at two lire.

RIDOLFO: Not all women are alike.

DON MARZIO: Women who roam around all over the place? Don't make me laugh!

RIDOLFO: Many respectable people go on pilgrimages. There's no way of knowing who a pilgrim like that may be.

DON MARZIO: I know her. She's the same one who was here last year.

RIDOLFO: I've never seen her before.

DON MARZIO: You're a dunce.

RIDOLFO: Thanks for the kind word. *(muttering to himself as he turns away to slap his napkin at a fly on the table)* How would you like me to comb that wig for you?

(Enter Eugenio from the gambling parlor, laughing happily.)

EUGENIO: Your servant, my lords and masters!

RIDOLFO: What! You here, Signor Eugenio?

DON MARZIO: Did you win?

EUGENIO: Indeed I did!

DON MARZIO: Wonder of wonders.

EUGENIO: What's so strange? Can't I win now and then? Am I half-witted?

RIDOLFO: Signor Eugenio, you swore off gambling!

EUGENIO: I won, didn't I?

RIDOLFO: What if you had lost?

EUGENIO: That couldn't happen—not today! I know when I'm going to lose. I feel it in my bones.

RIDOLFO: When you feel that way, why do you gamble?

EUGENIO: Because that's my day to lose.

RIDOLFO: When are you going home to your wife?

EUGENIO: Oh, get off my back!

RIDOLFO: I won't say another word. I'm wasting my breath.

(Enter Leandro from the gambling parlor.)

LEANDRO: What a man! He beat me! If I hadn't quit, he'd have wiped me out.

EUGENIO: Aha! Am I good or not? I won in three hands!

LEANDRO: He bets like a wild man.

EUGENIO: I bet like a real card-player!

Act II

DON MARZIO: *(to Leandro)* How much did he win?

LEANDRO: Plenty.

DON MARZIO: *(to Eugenio)* Tell me, what did you really win?

EUGENIO: *(gleefully)* Hey! Six ducats!

RIDOLFO: *(to himself)* The poor fool! Since yesterday he's lost a hundred and thirty, and he thinks he's won a fortune when he gets back six.

LEANDRO: *(aside)* Sometimes you have to bait the hook.

DON MARZIO: *(to Eugenio)* What do you intend to do with your six ducats?

EUGENIO: We could splurge on a big dinner.

DON MARZIO: Let's do.

RIDOLFO: *(to himself)* After all my work!

EUGENIO: Shall we go to the inn?

RIDOLFO: *(quietly to Eugenio)* Don't go there. They'll rope you into another game.

EUGENIO: *(quietly to Ridolfo)* Let 'em. Today's my lucky day.

RIDOLFO: *(to himself)* He's incurable.

LEANDRO: We could have dinner upstairs at Pandolfo's in the private room.

EUGENIO: Right! We'll order the meal at the inn and have them bring it up.

DON MARZIO: Excellent.

RIDOLFO: *(to himself)* Poor fool! He doesn't know what he's in for.

LEANDRO: Hey, Pandolfo!

(Pandolfo comes from the gambling parlor.)

PANDOLFO: Can I be of service?

LEANDRO: Would you let us use your private room upstairs for a little dinner?

PANDOLFO: You're always welcome, but I...I have rent to pay, you know.

LEANDRO: Naturally we'll compensate you for your trouble.

EUGENIO: Whatever it costs.

PANDOLFO: Very well, go right ahead. I'll get things ready. *(He goes into the gambling parlor.)*

EUGENIO: Now, who's going to order the meal?

LEANDRO: We'll leave it to you. You know your way around here.

DON MARZIO: Yes, you take charge of our dinner.

EUGENIO: What should I order?

LEANDRO: Whatever you like.

Act II

EUGENIO: You know the saying—we need wine, women, and song.

RIDOLFO: *(aside)* He wants women too!

DON MARZIO: The Count could bring along the little dancer.

LEANDRO: Yes, among friends I don't see why not.

DON MARZIO: *(to Leandro)* Is it true you're planning to marry her?

LEANDRO: This is not the time and place to discuss that.

EUGENIO: And I'll go get the pretty little pilgrim.

LEANDRO: What pilgrim is that?

EUGENIO: Oh, she's a lady, don't worry—very respectable.

DON MARZIO: *(to himself)* Oh yes? Have I got news for him!

LEANDRO: Well? Are you going to go order dinner?

EUGENIO: How many are we? The three of us, the two ladies, that's five; Don Marzio, have you a lady?

DON MARZIO: No, I'm with you.

EUGENIO: Ridolfo, will you have a bite with us?

RIDOLFO: Many thanks, but I have to tend shop.

EUGENIO: Now don't make us beg.

RIDOLFO: *(softly to Eugenio)* This is getting out of hand.

EUGENIO: I won some money, didn't I? I want to celebrate.

RIDOLFO: But afterwards—then what?

EUGENIO: Then—good night. I leave the future to fortune-tellers. *(He goes into the inn.)*

RIDOLFO: *(aside)* What's the use? I should have saved myself the trouble. *(He retreats into his shop.)*

DON MARZIO: Come on now, fetch your little dancer.

LEANDRO: I'll bring her when everything's ready.

DON MARZIO: Well, let's sit down. *(They sit.)* Have you been to the opera?

LEANDRO: Oh yes.

DON MARZIO: Did you like it?

LEANDRO: Very much.

DON MARZIO: You have deplorable taste. Where are you from?

LEANDRO: Torino.

DON MARZIO: An ugly city.

LEANDRO: On the contrary, it's considered one of the finest in Italy.

DON MARZIO: I'm Neapolitan. "See Naples and die."

LEANDRO: Here they say, "See Venice—then you can talk."

DON MARZIO: Do you have any snuff?

LEANDRO: *(offering his snuffbox)* Here's some. Help yourself.

Act II

DON MARZIO: That's terrible tobacco!

LEANDRO: I like it.

DON MARZIO: You're no connoisseur. The only real snuff is rapè.

LEANDRO: I like Spanish tobacco.

DON MARZIO: Spanish? It's vile.

LEANDRO: It's the best tobacco you can buy!

DON MARZIO: You're talking to an expert. *(vehemently)* Rapè, rapè! That's the only kind! Rapè!

LEANDRO: *(equally positive)* Yes, you're right—rapè is the best!

DON MARZIO: Not always. You have to discriminate, and you don't know what you're talking about!

(Eugenio returns from the inn.)

EUGENIO: What's all the fuss?

DON MARZIO: I yield to nobody when it comes to snuff!

LEANDRO: *(to Eugenio)* How's our meal coming along?

EUGENIO: It will soon be ready.

DON MARZIO: Is your pilgrim joining us?

EUGENIO: She won't come.

DON MARZIO: Well, Signor Snuff-lover, go get your lady.

LEANDRO: I will. *(to Eugenio)* If he behaves like this at the table, I'll throw my soup at him. That will wilt his mustache. *(He knocks at Lisaura's door.)*

DON MARZIO: Don't you have the key?

LEANDRO: No. *(The door opens and he goes in.)*

DON MARZIO: *(to Eugenio)* His key must be to the back door.

EUGENIO: I'm sorry the pilgrim decided not to come.

DON MARZIO: She only wants to be begged.

EUGENIO: She insists she has never been in Venice before.

DON MARZIO: She wouldn't dare say that to my face.

EUGENIO: Are you sure she's the same one?

DON MARZIO: Absolutely positive. I talked with her a little while ago and she wanted me to…! Well, enough said. Anyway, I didn't. I wouldn't betray an old friend that way.

EUGENIO: You spoke to her? And she recognized you?

DON MARZIO: Who doesn't? I'm very well known.

EUGENIO: In that case, why don't you go persuade her yourself?

DON MARZIO: If I go in person, she'll be overawed. You go and get her.

EUGENIO: She told me flatly she wouldn't come.

(Waiters from the inn are busily carrying tablecloth, napkins, plates,

Act II

silverware, wine, bread, glasses, and platters of food into Pandolfo's establishment.)

WAITER: Gentlemen, the soup's on. *(He goes into the gambling parlor with the others.)*

EUGENIO: *(to Don Marzio)* Where is the Count?

(Don Marzio knocks loudly at Lisaura's door.)

DON MARZIO: Up, up! On your feet in there! Assume the vertical! The soup's getting cold!

(Leandro comes out, giving a hand to Lisaura.)

LEANDRO: Here we are, here we are!

EUGENIO: *(to Lisaura)* Honored lady, my deepest respects.

DON MARZIO: *(quizzing her through his lorgnette)* Your slave.

LISAURA: Gentlemen, your humble servant.

EUGENIO: *(to Lisaura)* I'm delighted. You honor us with your company.

LISAURA: I came to please the Count.

DON MARZIO: And not us?

LISAURA: Especially not you.

DON MARZIO: The feeling is mutual. *(to Eugenio)* I wouldn't stoop to this kind of trash.

EUGENIO: *(to Lisaura)* Why don't you go in? Please sit down and start right away.

LISAURA: With your permission then. *(She goes into the gambling parlor with Leandro.)*

DON MARZIO: *(to Eugenio, lorgnette cocked at Lisaura)* Ooo! I never saw anything cheaper! *(He goes into the gambling parlor.)*

EUGENIO: Sour grapes. I wouldn't be so choosy. *(He follows them into the gambling parlor. Ridolfo comes from his shop.)*

RIDOLFO: There he goes, carousing while his wife suffers and sighs. Poor woman! My heart goes out to her.

(Eugenio, Don Marzio, Leandro, and Lisaura appear in the private room upstairs. They open the three windows and look down on the street.)

EUGENIO: *(at one window)* What a lovely day! Beautiful sunshine! Not at all cold.

DON MARZIO: *(at another window)* It's like spring.

LEANDRO: *(at the third window)* We can enjoy watching the passersby.

LISAURA: *(beside Leandro)* And the maskers in the carnival.

EUGENIO: Sit down, everybody! Sit down!

(They sit, Eugenio and Leandro near the windows. Trappola comes from the coffee shop.)

TRAPPOLA: *(to Ridolfo)* What's all the commotion?

RIDOLFO: That foolish Signor Eugenio! He's dining with Don Marzio and the Count and his dancer upstairs.

TRAPPOLA: *(looking up at the windows)* Good appetite, everyone!

Act II

EUGENIO: *(from his window)* Trappola, here's to you.

TRAPPOLA: Need a little help?

EUGENIO: Want to come up and serve the wine?

TRAPPOLA: I will if you'll give me a bite to eat.

EUGENIO: Come on up. We'll feed you.

TRAPPOLA: *(to Ridolfo)* If it's all right with you... *(He starts into the gambling parlor and is stopped by a waiter.)*

WAITER: Where are you going?

TRAPPOLA: To serve wine for my patrons.

WAITER: They don't need you. We're here for that.

TRAPPOLA: You a waiter, are you?

WAITER: Yes.

TRAPPOLA: Well, you just wait.

EUGENIO: Trappola, come on up.

TRAPPOLA: I'm coming! *(to the waiter)* See? *(He goes in.)*

WAITER: *(to another waiter)* Keep an eye on the platters. Don't let any outsiders snatch our left-overs. *(He goes into the inn.)*

RIDOLFO: How can people come into the world with so little sense? Signor Eugenio is determined to jump off the nearest cliff. Well, I did my best to save him, and I'll never be sorry for that.

EUGENIO: *(loudly)* Don Marzio! *(drinking)* A toast to this lady! Her health!

ALL: Your health! Your health!

(Vittoria, masked, enters and passes the coffee shop.)

RIDOLFO: Can I help you, lady masker? Can I be of service?

EUGENIO: *(drinking)* To the health of all good friends!

(Vittoria, looking for Eugenio, hears his voice, comes downstage the better to look up at the window, spots him, and is greatly agitated. Eugenio, not recognizing her, lifts his glass in a toast.)

And to you, masked lady! Would you like to join us?

(Vittoria trembles and shakes her head.)

You're welcome. We're all gentlemen here.

LISAURA: *(from the window)* Who's this masquerader you're inviting?

(Vittoria's agitation grows. Waiters come from the inn with more platters of food and take them into the gambling parlor.)

RIDOLFO: Who will pay for all this? The blockhead!

EUGENIO: *(to Vittoria)* If you don't want to come up, lady, it's all right with us. We have choicer ladies than you here.

VITTORIA: Oh God! I'm going to faint! That's the last straw!

RIDOLFO: *(to Vittoria)* Lady, are you feeling ill?

VITTORIA: *(removing her mask)* Ridolfo, in God's name help me!

Act II

RIDOLFO: You here? You need a little cordial! Come inside!

VITTORIA: I'll go up there and kill myself before his very eyes! I'll show the dirty dog!

RIDOLFO: Now, come in and calm down!

EUGENIO: *(drinking to Lisaura)* To the beautiful young woman with the splendid eyes!

VITTORIA: You hear the wretch? You hear him? Let me at him!

RIDOLFO: *(restraining her)* Let you kill yourself? Never! Not if I can help it!

VITTORIA: I can't bear this any more! Help me! I'm dying! *(She swoons.)*

RIDOLFO: This puts me in a pretty pickle! *(He does his best to support Vittoria's limp body. Placida appears at the door of the inn.)*

PLACIDA: Heavens! I thought I heard my husband's voice. If that's him up there, I'm just in time to expose him as a wife-deserter!

(A waiter comes from the gambling parlor, and she calls to him:)

Young man! Tell me, who is in the room up there?

WAITER: Signor Eugenio, Don Marzio the Neapolitan, and the Count Leandro Ardenti.

PLACIDA: You're sure it's not Flaminio? Perhaps he's changed his name.

LEANDRO: Here's to Eugenio and his winning streak!

ALL: *(toasting)* Here's to Eugenio! The winner!

PLACIDA: I know that voice! It's my husband! *(to the waiter)* Please, please take me up there! I have a little surprise for him!

WAITER: At your service. *(He takes her into the gambling parlor.)*

RIDOLFO: *(to Vittoria)* Be brave now. Everything will be all right.

VITTORIA: *(reviving)* I think I'll die!

(At the windows above, all rise from the table in alarm as Leandro, surprised by Placida's entrance, threatens her with his sword.)

EUGENIO: No! Stop!

DON MARZIO: Don't do that!

PLACIDA: Help, help! *(She runs for the stairs. Leandro tries to follow her, sword in hand, but Eugenio holds him back. Trappola, a napkinful of food in hand, leaps from a window and disappears into the coffee shop. Placida comes running from the gambling parlor and flees into the inn. Eugenio has drawn his sword in defense of Placida against Leandro, who is pursuing his wife. Don Marzio very quietly sneaks away from the brawl. Trappola pokes his head from the coffee shop to watch.)*

DON MARZIO: *Rumores fuge.*

TRAPPOLA: That's Latin—"rumor is fudge."

DON MARZIO: *(turning back momentarily to correct him)* It means "Stay out of stampedes!"

(The waiters scamper wildly from the gambling parlor and lock themselves in the inn. Vittoria remains in the coffee shop supported by Ridolfo.)

Act II

LEANDRO: *(sword drawn, to Eugenio)* Get out of the way! I'm after her!

EUGENIO: Your own wife? I'll save her from you if it takes the last drop of my blood!

LEANDRO: *(brandishing his sword)* By God, you'll be sorry!

EUGENIO: I'm not afraid of you! *(He attacks Leandro and forces him to retreat until, finding Lisaura's door open, Leandro escapes inside. Eugenio rages at him through the closed door.)* You dirty coward! Come on out and fight like a man!

VITTORIA: *(thrusting herself in Eugenio's path)* If you want blood, spill mine!

EUGENIO: Get out of here, you brainless…woman!

VITTORIA: You'll never get rid of me alive, so kill me!

EUGENIO: *(threatening her with the sword)* Get out, damn it, or I will!

(Ridolfo grabs a chair and comes to Vittoria's defense.)

RIDOLFO: Just because you've got a sword you think you can scare everybody? You mistreat this poor lady—and now you threaten her? She may be defenseless, but I'll protect her! *(to Vittoria)* Come with me! Don't be afraid!

VITTORIA: No, Ridolfo, let him kill me! Let the beast satisfy his lust for blood! Go on, kill me, you dog! Butcher me, you miserable wretch! You're a disgrace to humankind!

(Eugenio, shamefaced, sheathes his sword in silence.)

RIDOLFO: Ah, Signor Eugenio, I apologize; I spoke out of turn. But this poor lady breaks my heart. Don't her tears touch you?

(Eugenio wipes his eyes and is silent.) Look, Signora Vittoria, he's crying! He'll change his ways!

VITTORIA: Crocodile tears! How many times he's promised to change! How many times he's fooled me! I don't believe him any more!

(Eugenio trembles with shame and fury. Like a madman he throws his cap on the ground and stalks into the coffee shop without a word.)

Why doesn't he say something? Why doesn't he answer me?

RIDOLFO: He's ashamed. He would like to apologize, but he doesn't know how.

VITTORIA: Oh, Ridolfo, let's go comfort him!

RIDOLFO: You'll have to do that on your own.

VITTORIA: You go to him first and see how he is.

RIDOLFO: I expect he'll be very sorry. *(He goes into the coffee shop.)*

VITTORIA: This is the last time he sees me weep. Either he apologizes or I leave him cold.

(Ridolfo returns.)

RIDOLFO: He's gone! He left by the back door! *(picking up Eugenio's cap)* Look, he went without his cap. He doesn't know what he's doing.

VITTORIA: If he's sorry, why didn't he say so?

RIDOLFO: Maybe he was afraid to.

VITTORIA: Oh, he knows how easy it is to wheedle forgiveness out of a foolish wife like me!

RIDOLFO: He's ashamed.

VITTORIA: Ridolfo, now you're wheedling me!

RIDOLFO: Go into my back room while I look for him. I'll send him running back to you like a little puppy dog.

VITTORIA: Better to forget about him!

RIDOLFO: Do it my way, just this once!

VITTORIA: All right, I'll wait for half an hour so I can say I did everything I could to get my husband back. But he'd better not take advantage of my generosity. *(She goes into the coffee shop.)*

RIDOLFO: If he were my own son I couldn't go to more trouble for him. *(He leaves.)*

(Lisaura comes from the gambling parlor alone, first making sure there is nobody in sight.)

LISAURA: That worthless Count! He led me on to believe he would marry me—when he already had a wife! We women are too gullible; I fell for being a countess. I should have stuck to dancing! *(She goes into her place and locks the door.)*

ACT III

Scene: The same.

At rise: Lisaura is chasing Leandro from her door.

LISAURA: *(brandishing a broom in the doorway)* You fake! You liar!

LEANDRO: What did I do? I left my wife for you, didn't I?

LISAURA: If I had known, you'd never have got inside this door!

LEANDRO: I wasn't the first!

LISAURA: You'll be the last!

(Don Marzio enters and watches through his lorgnette, enjoying the spectacle.)

LEANDRO: You were well paid for your time!

LISAURA: I'm ashamed I ever shared your winnings, you cheat! Go to the devil—and stay away from me!

LEANDRO: My things are in there! I want them back! *(She goes in and slams the door.)* You can't treat me this way! You'll pay, you hear?

(Don Marzio laughs, but when Leandro turns at the sound, he quickly assumes a grave expression.)

Did you see that?

DON MARZIO: See what? I just came in.

LEANDRO: You didn't see the dancer—at her door there—just now?

Act III

DON MARZIO: No. What happened? You can tell me. I'm an outsider here like yourself, but I know these people better than you do. If you need help or advice, I'm your man.

LEANDRO: If I confide in you, will you keep it quiet?

DON MARZIO: Trust me.

LEANDRO: That pilgrim woman is my wife. I left her in Torino.

DON MARZIO: *(staring at Leandro through his lorgnette)* You rascal, you!

LEANDRO: My name's not Leandro, and I'm not a Count.

DON MARZIO: *(still staring through his lorgnette)* This gets better and better. You're not an undercover policeman, are you?

LEANDRO: Please! I may not be noble but I'm honest! I used to work as a merchant's clerk...

DON MARZIO: Much too fatiguing, am I right?

LEANDRO: ...yes, and wishing to see the world...

DON MARZIO: ...at somebody else's expense...

LEANDRO: ...I came to Venice...

DON MARZIO: ...to be a cardsharp.

LEANDRO: What? Are you calling me names?

DON MARZIO: As your confidant, I reserve the right to comment now and then.

LEANDRO: You can see the spot I'm in if my wife discloses who I am.

DON MARZIO: What do you plan to do about her?

LEANDRO: Couldn't she be run out of Venice as a tramp?

DON MARZIO: Now, now! You really are a rascal!

LEANDRO: How do you mean that?

DON MARZIO: As your friend and confidant.

LEANDRO: Or I could leave town before she can denounce me to the authorities. Do you think I should?

DON MARZIO: Oh yes, your best bet is to leave at once. Take a gondola as far as Fusina, catch the coach and go to Ferrara.

LEANDRO: I'll leave as soon as it's dark. First I want to retrieve a few of my things from the dancer's.

DON MARZIO: Then hurry. And don't let anybody see you.

LEANDRO: I'll use the back door.

DON MARZIO: I knew it! I said all along you used the back door!

LEANDRO: Remember—not a word to anybody. Absolute secrecy.

DON MARZIO: Depend on it.

LEANDRO: Do me a favor—give my wife these two ducats to get home on. *(giving Don Marzio the coins)* Write me as soon as she's gone and I'll sneak back to Venice.

DON MARZIO: I'll give them to her. Go now. Hurry.

LEANDRO: But make sure she really leaves.

Act III

DON MARZIO: Go, go, confound you!

LEANDRO: Are you trying to get rid of me?

DON MARZIO: I'm telling you, as a friend, for your own good—go before the devil catches up with you!

LEANDRO: What kind of friendly talk is that? *(He goes into Lisaura's.)*

DON MARZIO: A Count! It's a good thing the scoundrel confided in me, or I'd break every bone in his body!

(Placida enters from the inn.)

Lady pilgrim, how goes it?

PLACIDA: You! You were at dinner with my husband, weren't you?

DON MARZIO: Yes, I'm the man with the dried nuts. Chestnuts.

PLACIDA: For the love of heaven, tell me where that wife-betrayer is.

DON MARZIO: Go back to Torino and forget your husband. You're better off without him.

PLACIDA: That may be, but I must talk to him before I go.

DON MARZIO: You'll never see him again.

PLACIDA: Why do you say that? You must know something!

DON MARZIO: Yes—but my lips are sealed. Go home and forget him. Here, I'll give you two ducats.

PLACIDA: Heaven reward your kindness! *(as she is about to go)* Can't you tell me anything about my husband?

DON MARZIO: Poor woman... *(calling)* Hey! Your husband's at the dancer's, getting his things. He'll sneak out by the back door. *(He goes out.)*

PLACIDA: So he's with that dancer! If I try to talk to him, I'm afraid he might beat me.

(Ridolfo and Eugenio enter.)

EUGENIO: My wife won't believe me any more.

RIDOLFO: She loves you! Everything will work out!

PLACIDA: Signor Eugenio?

RIDOLFO: Let him be. He has other worries on his mind.

PLACIDA: I hate to bother him, but I'm in trouble. Won't anyone listen?

EUGENIO: Believe me, Ridolfo, this poor woman deserves compassion. She's completely honest, though her husband's a scoundrel.

PLACIDA: He abandoned me. When I finally found him here in Venice, he tried to kill me. Now he wants to slip away again.

RIDOLFO: Where is he?

PLACIDA: There, at the dancer's, gathering his belongings. He intends to sneak out the back. If he sees me, he'll kill me.

RIDOLFO: Who told you he'll go out the back?

PLACIDA: Don Marzio.

RIDOLFO: Oh, the town cryer! Here—go into the barber shop. From there you can see the secret door at the back. When he comes out, call me. I'll deal with him.

PLACIDA: They won't allow a woman in the barber shop.

RIDOLFO: Wait a minute. *(calling)* Hey, Messer Agabito!

(The barber's apprentice comes out of the shop.)

BARBER'S APPRENTICE: Did you call, Messer Ridolfo?

RIDOLFO: Ask your master to keep this pilgrim lady in the shop for a little while, till I come and get her.

BARBER'S APPRENTICE: Gladly. Come with me, lady, and I'll show you the art of the close shave. But you probably know more about clipping a man than we do. *(He returns to the barber shop.)*

PLACIDA: Nothing but insults! All because of my worthless husband! It's better to jump in the canal than marry a man like mine. *(She goes into the barber shop.)*

RIDOLFO: I'd like to help that poor pilgrim get out of town. Then your wife will have no cause to be jealous. How are you going to handle your wife? Would you like me to go with you to the back room and talk to her?

EUGENIO: No, no, you'll make her self-conscious. Of course, if I go in alone she'll scratch my eyes out… But never mind, let her get it out of her system. I'll go in alone.

RIDOLFO: Go then—and God be with you.

EUGENIO: If I need you, I'll shout. Well, here I go. *(He starts out.)*

RIDOLFO: Be brave.

EUGENIO: *(turning back)* What do you think she'll do—cry, or scratch?

RIDOLFO: She'll try everything.

EUGENIO: What do I do?

RIDOLFO: You'll think of something.

EUGENIO: Don't come in unless I really yell for help.

RIDOLFO: Go on. Go to her.

EUGENIO: Ridolfo, you're a true friend. *(He goes into the back of the coffee shop.)*

RIDOLFO: Husbands and wives! Let 'em work it out for themselves. Hey, Trappola! Boys! Where are you?

(Enter Trappola.)

TRAPPOLA: Here I am.

RIDOLFO: Mind the shop while I go to the barber's. If Signor Eugenio calls for me, give me a shout and I'll come running.

TRAPPOLA: Shall I go in and keep them company?

RIDOLFO: No! Don't you go in there! And make sure nobody else does.

TRAPPOLA: Why not?

RIDOLFO: Because!

TRAPPOLA: I just want to see if he needs anything, or anything.

Act III

RIDOLFO: Don't go in unless he calls. I want to check on the pilgrim lady. *(He goes into the barber shop.)*

TRAPPOLA: *(his curiosity aroused)* Why doesn't he want me to go in? What's going on in there?

(Don Marzio enters quietly and startles Trappola as he is peeking in the door.)

DON MARZIO: Did I frighten you? Have you seen Eugenio?

TRAPPOLA: Sh! He's inside.

DON MARZIO: Where?

TRAPPOLA: Sh! In the back room.

DON MARZIO: What's he doing? Playing cards?

TRAPPOLA: *(snickering)* Well, he's playing, all right!

DON MARZIO: Who else is in the game?

TRAPPOLA: *(whispering)* His wife.

DON MARZIO: His wife's in there?

TRAPPOLA: Yes. Sh!

DON MARZIO: I'm going in to see him.

TRAPPOLA: Not allowed.

DON MARZIO: Why not?

TRAPPOLA: The boss says so.

DON MARZIO: *(starting in)* Oh, get out of my way, you clown!

TRAPPOLA: *(blocking his way)* I tell you—you can't go in.

DON MARZIO: *(trying to get by him)* I tell you—I will!

TRAPPOLA: And I tell you—you won't.

DON MARZIO: I'll take a stick to you!

    (Ridolfo comes from the barber shop.)

RIDOLFO: What's going on?

TRAPPOLA: He's trying to force his way between husband and wife.

RIDOLFO: Calm down, Don Marzio. Nobody goes in there.

DON MARZIO: I insist!

RIDOLFO: In my shop I give the orders. Behave yourself or I'll call in the law. *(to Trappola and Giovanni)* Don't you boys let anybody in, I don't care who it is. *(He knocks at Lisaura's door and goes in.)*

TRAPPOLA: Hear that? Pay some respect to matrimony.

DON MARZIO: *(pacing up and down)* Pay respect? Me? You filthy swine! *(sitting at a table)* Bring me some coffee!

TRAPPOLA: Right away. *(He goes for coffee and serves it to Don Marzio. Pandolfo enters.)*

PANDOLFO: Excellency, I need your help.

DON MARZIO: Ah, the gambling man. Well, what is it?

Act III

PANDOLFO: It's something very distressing. It's...

DON MARZIO: What's wrong? Confide in me. I'll help you, my good man.

PANDOLFO: There are envious people in the world—malicious people who hate to have a poor man succeed. They see me struggling to feed my family, and these scoundrels report me to the police. They accuse me of cheating at cards.

DON MARZIO: *(sarcastically)* An honest man like you? How did you find out about it?

PANDOLFO: A friend in the constable's office warned me. But I'm sure they have no proof. There's never been a breath of scandal about me.

DON MARZIO: I could tell some fine stories about you.

PANDOLFO: Excellency, I beg you! For the love of heaven, don't ruin me! For the sake of my poor little children!

DON MARZIO: All right, I'll help you. Do you have any marked cards on the premises?

PANDOLFO: I never mark cards myself, but some customers do.

DON MARZIO: Quick, burn them at once.

PANDOLFO: There's no time to burn anything!

DON MARZIO: Then hide them.

PANDOLFO: I will. I'll go hide them now.

DON MARZIO: Have you a good safe place?

PANDOLFO: Absolutely safe. Under the beams. The devil himself couldn't find them. *(He hurries into his gambling parlor.)*

DON MARZIO: Well, you are a sly one.

(Enter the Chief Constable, in plain clothes, with other Constables, who lurk in corners.)

He's a jailbird if ever there was one. If they discover half of his felonies, they'll have him in irons for life.

(The Chief Constable signals to the other Constables, and they disperse around the corner.)

CHIEF CONSTABLE: Check out the neighborhood, and when I whistle come running.

DON MARZIO: Marked cards! What cheats people are!

CHIEF CONSTABLE: *(sitting down)* Coffee!

TRAPPOLA: At once. *(He goes for coffee and serves the Chief Constable.)*

CHIEF CONSTABLE: Fine weather we're having.

DON MARZIO: It won't last.

CHIEF CONSTABLE: Never mind. If the weather turns bad, you can always go to a casino and play a game or two.

DON MARZIO: If they don't cheat you blind.

CHIEF CONSTABLE: This place seems reputable enough.

DON MARZIO: Reputable? It's a den of thieves.

Act III

CHIEF CONSTABLE: Messer Pandolfo runs it, I believe.

DON MARZIO: He's the man all right.

CHIEF CONSTABLE: Frankly, I hear he's a bit slippery.

DON MARZIO: He's an out-and-out swindler.

CHIEF CONSTABLE: Has he tricked you too?

DON MARZIO: Me? I'm no fool! But whoever walks in there is a plucked duck.

CHIEF CONSTABLE: He must suspect something; he's nowhere to be seen.

DON MARZIO: He's inside, hiding cards.

CHIEF CONSTABLE: Hiding cards? Why?

DON MARZIO: Because they're marked, wouldn't you suppose?

CHIEF CONSTABLE: I see. But—hiding them where?

DON MARZIO: Want a good laugh? He hides them under the beams.

CHIEF CONSTABLE: *(rising)* That's all I need to know.

DON MARZIO: You like to gamble?

CHIEF CONSTABLE: *(finishing his coffee)* Upon occasion.

DON MARZIO: I don't believe I know you.

CHIEF CONSTABLE: *(putting down the cup)* You soon will.

DON MARZIO: You're leaving?

CHIEF CONSTABLE: I'll be back.

TRAPPOLA: *(to the Chief Constable)* Hey! The coffee!

CHIEF CONSTABLE: I'll pay you later. *(He goes into the street and whistles. The Constables rush around the corner and into the gambling parlor. Don Marzio and Trappola watch attentively.)*

DON MARZIO: Trappola...

TRAPPOLA: Don Marzio?

DON MARZIO: Who are these men?

TRAPPOLA: I think they're undercover police.

(The Constables bring out Pandolfo, shackled.)

PANDOLFO: Much obliged, Don Marzio!

DON MARZIO: I don't know what you're talking about.

PANDOLFO: I may go to jail, but your tongue deserves even worse! *(He is led off by the Constables.)*

CHIEF CONSTABLE: *(to Don Marzio)* You were right. I found him hiding his marked cards. *(He leaves.)*

TRAPPOLA: I'll go see where they take him. *(He follows them off.)*

DON MARZIO: The devil! I thought that man was a gentleman—and he turns out to be a policeman! He deceived me.

(Ridolfo and Leandro come from Lisaura's.)

RIDOLFO: *(to Leandro)* Good! When a man acknowledges he was in the wrong, he shows he's a real man.

LEANDRO: There's the one who told me to clear out.

RIDOLFO: Fine advice, Don Marzio! Instead of trying to reunite him with his wife, you tell him to leave her in the lurch again?

DON MARZIO: Reunite him with his wife? Impossible! He can't stand her.

RIDOLFO: It wasn't impossible for me. I persuaded him in two minutes. He's going back home with her.

LEANDRO: *(aside)* I have to, or I'm sunk.

RIDOLFO: Let's go get her. She's at the barber's.

DON MARZIO: *(to Leandro)* Yes, go get that wife of yours. A fine piece of goods she is!

LEANDRO: Don Marzio, let me tell you in confidence, you have a long poisonous tongue. *(He goes into the barber shop with Ridolfo.)*

DON MARZIO: Now and then my tongue may say something this person or that doesn't like to hear, but I'll never squelch it as long as I believe it's telling the truth. I freely tell what I know because I'm an open-hearted and generous man.

(Ridolfo comes from the barber shop.)

RIDOLFO: Well, that's done. If he's sincere, he truly regrets what he did to her; and if he's pretending, he's stuck with her now.

DON MARZIO: The great Ridolfo—the marriage counselor! The reconciler of couples drifting apart!

RIDOLFO: And you're the man who splits them up.

DON MARZIO: I do it for their own good.

RIDOLFO: Nothing good can come of deliberately separating husband and wife.

DON MARZIO: *(scornfully)* You're a fine lecturer!

RIDOLFO: Don Marzio, you may be better educated than I am; but my tongue is under better control.

DON MARZIO: You are insolent.

RIDOLFO: Then forgive me if you can; and if you cannot, take your business elsewhere.

DON MARZIO: I certainly shall! I'll never come to this shop of yours again!

RIDOLFO: Thank you.

(Giovanni comes from the coffee shop.)

GIOVANNI: *(to Ridolfo)* Signor Eugenio would like to see you. *(He goes.)*

RIDOLFO: I'll be right with him. *(to Don Marzio)* By your leave.

DON MARZIO: I salute the Master Diplomat. What do you expect to gain by these shenanigans of yours?

RIDOLFO: Friends and respect. They're worth more to me than anything in the world. *(He goes into his shop.)*

Act III

DON MARZIO: What a madman! Delusions of grandeur—a man who runs a coffee shop!

(Ridolfo, Eugenio, and Vittoria come from the coffee shop.)

The three lunatics—the crazy prodigal, the jealous madwoman, and the megalomaniac.

VITTORIA: Dear Ridolfo, I owe you everything—my peace of mind, my whole life!

EUGENIO: Believe me, my friend, I was fed up with the way I was living, but I didn't know how to quit. You opened my eyes, and I trust this change will last—as a testimonial to you, a wise and honest man.

RIDOLFO: You overwhelm me. I don't deserve such praise.

VITTORIA: As long as I live I'll remember it was you who restored my dear husband to me. When I became his bride I shed a few tears, and God knows how many when I lost him. Now getting him back is costing me more tears than ever. But these are sweet tears of love that wash out all the past unhappiness. I thank heaven—and you.

RIDOLFO: You're making me cry.

DON MARZIO: *(waving his lorgnette)* What damned fools!

EUGENIO: Shall we go home?

VITTORIA: I hate to have them see me, blubbering like this. My mother will be there. Ridolfo, do you have a mirror?

DON MARZIO: *(staring at her through his lorgnette)* Her husband has mussed up her hairdo.

RIDOLFO: There's a mirror upstairs above the gambling den.

EUGENIO: I never want to set foot in that place again!

RIDOLFO: Haven't you heard—Pandolfo's been arrested.

EUGENIO: Serves him right.

VITTORIA: Let's go upstairs, dear.

EUGENIO: Well, as long as nobody's there—all right.

VITTORIA: I can't let them see me at home in such a state. *(She goes gaily into the gambling parlor.)*

EUGENIO: *(following her off)* Poor old girl! She's bubbling over with joy.

RIDOLFO: I'll show you where the mirror is. *(He follows them off.)*

DON MARZIO: Eugenio made up with his wife because he's broke and has no other merchandise. She's young and pretty, and Ridolfo will do the pimping for him.

(Leandro and Placida come from the barber shop.)

LEANDRO: Let's go to the inn and pick up your belongings.

PLACIDA: Darling, how could you ever have abandoned me like that?

LEANDRO: Forget it. I promised to change my ways, didn't I?

PLACIDA: I hope to heaven you will. *(She goes toward the inn.)*

DON MARZIO: *(mocking Leandro)* Your humble servant, most illustrious Count!

Act III

LEANDRO: Ah! Old Signor Slimy Tongue himself!

DON MARZIO: I bow low before my lady Countess.

PLACIDA: Your servant, Sir Knight of the Dried Nuts. *(She goes into the inn with Leandro.)*

DON MARZIO: Now they'll both become pilgrims. They've nothing to their names but a pack of cards.

(Lisaura appears at her window.)

LISAURA: There she is with that wretch Leandro. If she stays, I'm leaving. I can't stand the sight of her, or him either.

DON MARZIO: *(employing his lorgnette)* Your servant, dancing lady.

LISAURA: *(shortly)* Greetings.

DON MARZIO: What's the matter? You seem upset.

LISAURA: I'm surprised the innkeeper takes in such people.

DON MARZIO: Who?

LISAURA: That pilgrim woman. She's nothing but a common hussy. We've never had such trash in the neighborhood before.

(Placida appears in the window of the inn.)

PLACIDA: Hey! Are you talking about me? I'm a respectable woman, whatever you may be.

LISAURA: Respectable women don't gallivant all over the country.

(Don Marzio, lorgnette waving, looks from one to the other, laughing.)

PLACIDA: I came to get my husband.

LISAURA: Oh yes? Who was it last year?

PLACIDA: I wasn't here last year! I've never been in Venice before in my life!

LISAURA: Liar! At the last carnival you were the laughingstock of the whole town.

(Don Marzio is convulsed with laughter.)

PLACIDA: Who says so?

LISAURA: Don Marzio there—he told me.

DON MARZIO: I never said anything of the kind!

PLACIDA: He couldn't have spread such a brazen lie! But he told me about all the customers you let in at the back door.

DON MARZIO: I never said that! *(He stares at them in turn through his lorgnette.)*

PLACIDA: Oh yes you did!

LISAURA: Don Marzio said a nasty thing like that?

DON MARZIO: I swear I didn't!

(Eugenio appears above at one window, Ridolfo at another, and Vittoria at the third.)

Act III

EUGENIO: That's what he said about both of you. The pilgrim lady was here in Venice last year, up to no good, he told me. And the dancer let men in at the back door.

DON MARZIO: I heard that from Ridolfo!

RIDOLFO: From me? Never! I said Signora Lisaura was a respectable lady and your excellency insisted she was not.

LISAURA: Oh, the wretch!

DON MARZIO: Ridolfo's a liar!

VITTORIA: Don Marzio said you were both hussies.

PLACIDA: Disgraceful!

LISAURA: Ah, you damned...!

(Leandro appears at the inn door.)

LEANDRO: Yes! Yes! A gentleman! Smearing the names of two honorable ladies with your filthy tongue!

DON MARZIO: You call the dancer a lady?

LISAURA: Yes, I am! I expected to marry Leandro. I didn't know he already had a wife.

PLACIDA: Well, he has! Me!

LEANDRO: If I had listened to Don Marzio, I'd have skipped out again.

PLACIDA: The worthless busybody!

LISAURA: The meddler!

VITTORIA: Slanderer!

EUGENIO: Blabber-mouth!

DON MARZIO: Me? The only respectable man around? I never committed a dishonorable act in my life!

(Trappola comes forward.)

TRAPPOLA: Oh, Don Marzio, you committed a beauty!

RIDOLFO: What did he do?

TRAPPOLA: He informed on Messer Pandolfo.

RIDOLFO: Informed? On Pandolfo?

TRAPPOLA: Yes, the constables have nabbed him and they say he'll be flogged in public tomorrow.

RIDOLFO: An informer? Get out of my shop! *(He leaves the window. The barber's apprentice enters.)*

BARBER'S APPRENTICE: Signor Informer, don't come into our shop again for a shave! *(He returns to the barber shop. The waiter comes from the inn.)*

WAITER: Signor Informer, don't come to our inn any more for your dinner! *(He returns to the inn.)*

LEANDRO: Signor Lecher—confidentially, informing is a nasty business! *(He goes into the inn and slams the door.)*

PLACIDA: You and your dried nuts! Signor Stool Pigeon! *(She slams her window.)*

Act III

LISAURA: Hang him! To the gallows with him! *(She slams her window.)*

VITTORIA: Dear Don Marzio, those ten ducats you lent my husband—were they a reward for your informing? *(She slams her window.)*

EUGENIO: Goodbye, Signor Loose Mouth! *(He slams his window.)*

TRAPPOLA: My respects, Signor Snitch! *(He goes into the coffee shop and slams the door.)*

DON MARZIO: I'm astonished. An informer—me? Because I mention Pandolfo's shady deals, just casually? How did I know I was talking to an undercover policeman? Nobody in this town will have anything to do with me now. I'll have to get out of here. But I'll leave with regret. This miserable tongue of mine has driven me from a place where all enjoy life and liberty, and peace and pleasure, as long as they know enough to keep their mouths shut.

END OF PLAY

Note

Latin lovers should be reassured that Trappola's version of the dead language of the Romans is his own invention; and Don Marzio's is perhaps a dim recollection from his schooldays.

For Trappola's Latin phrase toward the beginning of Act II, Goldoni has "*lupus est in fabula*" (the wolf is in the fable). Trappola intends to say *lupus in fabula,* a Latin idiom we would translate as "speak of the devil!" But when asked what it means, Trappola puts it into terrible Italian: "*Il lupo pesta la fava*" (the wolf stamps on the bean). None of this would make the slightest sense in English, and any joke involved would simply die and leave the hearer befuddled. So this translator changes the Latin to *forte dux in aero,* roughly the equivalent of "mighty leader clad in armor." To Trappola, of course, it means "forty ducks in a row."

The second Latin phrase is spoken by Don Marzio as he tries to escape from the brawl inside the gambling den toward the end of Act II: "*Rumores fuge.*" It can mean "avoid loud noises," or "shun popular opinion," or "run away from hearsay," among other things. What it does not mean is "rumor is fudge," as Trappola contends. "Stay out of stampedes," as Don Marzio would have it, is somewhat closer.

Since Latin has dropped out of most school curricula in the last couple of generations, a director might want to let these two lines of Latin drop from *The Coffee Shop* as well.

—*Robert Cornthwaite*